Karahee from the Cane Fields

Rajiv Mohabir
GUEST EDITOR

S. Shankar
SERIES EDITOR

CONTENTS

Photograph by Andil Gosine

Editor's Note

Welcome to a new edition of *Mānoa: A Pacific Journal of International Writing*, my first as editor of the journal. There have been a few changes at the journal in the last few years. Frank Stewart, who edited so ably for more than thirty years, retired from the journal a little more than a year ago and was succeeded by poet and critic Craig Santos Perez. Craig served as editor for a year and facilitated the last two exciting issues on CHamoru literature and eco-writing. As I assume this role for the next (three-year) term, I look forward to seeing through a transition in a journal that has played such a prominent role over the decades in bringing attention to the vibrant and diverse literatures of the Pacific, Asia, and the Americas. The transition will involve innovations—about which I will say more in future issues—while also preserving the enduring work of previous editors and the tradition of literary excellence in English and in translation for which the journal is rightly known.

I bring to my role as editor a particular interest in the postcolonial world, especially South Asia and Africa. I am the author of three novels (largely set in India), two volumes of criticism, and several shorter journalistic and scholarly pieces. I am also a translator from Tamil, and I view translation, which has been central to *Mānoa* over the decades and about which I have written extensively in a scholarly mode, as an infinitely variable and interesting literary and cultural phenomenon. While my approach as editor will no doubt be shaped by my commitments and experiences as a writer, critic, and translator, I will rely on the editorial and advisory boards for vital input in shaping the journal.

Joining me in taking the journal through the transition and beyond is Amanda Galvan Huynh, Managing Editor. Amanda succeeds Pat Matsueda in this role. Alongside Frank, Pat was a presence in *Mānoa* over the decades, the indispensable hand on the levers of the day-to-day machinery of the journal. She left the journal at the same time as Frank for a well-deserved retirement. Amanda and I are keen to preserve Pat's fine legacy in the journal while working to ensure a smooth transition.

I could not ask for a better managing editor to work with than Amanda, whose commitment and skill are already evident in this issue that you view on your screen or hold in your hands. Amanda is the author of a poetry collection, a poetry chapbook, a coedited volume on poetics, and numerous poems and essays in journals. She has a particular interest in multilingual poetics. *Mānoa* deserves a visionary and capable managing editor dedicated to international literature and literary excellence, and Amanda is certainly that person.

This issue has also benefited from the work and support of other people. Audrey Beaton, Anna Kalabukhova, Chandanie Somwaru, and Mia Winand—the four interns at the journal—are part of the *Mānoa* team, adroitly assisting Amanda and me in putting this issue together and making it available to our readers. Mānoa Center for the Humanities and Civic Engagement (MCHACE) and the Center for South Asian Studies (CSAS), both at the University of Hawai'i at Mānoa, have supported the publication of this issue monetarily. Their timely assistance has been crucial for the gorgeousness with which the material in the special issue is presented to you. We are deeply grateful to Brandy Nālani McDougall, Director of MCHACE, and Anna Stirr, Director of CSAS. I would also like to thank Sai Bhatawadekar, professor of Hindi here at the University of Hawai'i at Mānoa, for assistance with the Hindi/Bhojpuri that appears in Devanagari script on various pages.

And how delicious are the pages of this issue, guest edited by Rajiv Mohabir, an extraordinary poet and savant of multiple genres! *Karahee from the Cane Fields: Writing from the Coolie Diaspora* brings together a diverse set of literary works, mostly in original English but also in translation from Hindi, Bhojpuri, Tamil, and French, as well as art from communities of South Asian descent in the Caribbean, Africa, the Indian Ocean, and the Pacific formed by the outmigration of indentured laborers from the British colony of India in the nineteenth and early twentieth centuries. Rajiv's splendid introduction, written out of deep personal experience and broad, rigorous learning, maps this literary community with insight, intuition, meticulousness, and feeling. It also offers necessary context for the literary and artistic works presented and for the term *coolie*, about which there has been debate.

Powerfully affecting retellings of indentured ancestry as well as stirring statements of reimagined futures—they are all here in this issue, a delicious dish cooked out of the past and the future in the karahee of the present.

S. Shankar
Honolulu, Hawai'i

RAJIV MOHABIR

On Organizing the Coolie's Karahee: The Diaspora's New Literary Directions

"You're Indian? Where from?" Answering this, I never had words like Gujarati, Bengali, Punjabi, Tamil, Malayali, Assamese, Kashmiri, or Sindhi. Rather, I had "Guyanese." My parents' fridge was always packed with empty yogurt containers filled with things like beans and potatoes. I look at my hands. They've always been called "East Indian," but "India" was never a home in any recent memory. According to family stories—sitting at my Aja's brother's side or reading my Nana's autobiography—I have discovered that my family left India in 1890 and 1885. They crossed the Kala Pani—a metaphor that haunts me today. This crossing of the "black waters" was to erase themselves from their ancestral lands, to disappear the ancestors and rishis from whom they descended. Crossing the Kala Pani was to allow the dark cloud of erasure a home in the chest. No more caste. No more kin. My ancestors were bound to serve the British East India Company for at least five years of labor, followed by a reneged promise of return to India.

About life before their thumbprints signed contracts, there's not much familial memory. Most of my ancestors left from Kolkata, then Calcutta, and some from Chennai, then Madras. I don't know who spoke what language or which castes were represented. What were their gotras? I don't know what ethnicities they claimed, which hills were sacred to whom, or in which fields their navel strings were buried. Were any of my ancestors "Hill Coolies," Adivasi—indigenous? I imagine the first contact that these people had in the loading docks, beginning to galvanize a lingua franca—a koine language—of mutually intelligible sounds and prayers of safe return from their incredible diverse beginnings. There was no one Indian. There still isn't, at least in India, nor in the different South Asian diasporas.

When my ancestors came to the Caribbean, they went through a process of Creolization and Koinization that was site-specific. Koinization is a linguistic process where North Indian languages coalesce to form a language variety that is mutually intelligible. We didn't start out as one people from one place. Empire made us into *Indians*, into *Coolies*. We worked to be legible to one another. It's through the homogenizing of state and colonial approaches that we were written into one ontological whole—ironically fragmenting us further, barring us from alliances and coalitions with our siblings, who endured similar treatment and were dehumanized under British hands.

What is important is the consideration of the mythic webs we wend to bring us into this present space—a time where we remain indentured, whether through student loans, the glass ceilings of a capitalist meritocracy illusion, or the new forced migration arising from American consumerism and the global economy. We are at a time where we are doing the same, arriving into a new space. This time we are coming from various nations, learning to speak a mutual language—showing each other the white scars we bear, rising from British whips.

The cover image by the Trinidadian artist Renluka Maharaj shows a photo taken of a woman indentured from British India and shipped to the Caribbean to be exploited for her labor on the sugar cane fields. In the foreground of this piece called "Lalika's Daydream 2023," a sugarcane stalk grows out of the frame. This piece speaks to the communities of people descended of Coolie indentured labor, as through the use of added color, patterns, and texture, the past is literally reenvisioned and made beautiful through a woman artist's reclamation of her history, her rereading it, and presenting it with new life, asking the question now of who is beholding whom: the power of the camera being wrested back into the reddened hands, reddened through the biting leaves of cane and decoration, of a surviving descendant. This image offers a deep framing of the writing and art assembled in this issue titled *Karahee from the Cane Fields: Writing from the Coolie Diaspora*—how the writers assembled add color and texture to the stories and songs after their ancestral surviving of indenture.

I would not spell the word "karahee" as N. Nardina Bi spells it in their piece; rather, I would err on the side of "kardhai," which betrays the Creolese (Guyanese English Creole) pronunciation of this wok-shaped pot in which we fry, bhunje, paache, and boil ingredients to create nourishing foods. The karahee, and Bi's spelling itself, is iconic to Coolie cuisine, descended of foodways from South Asia that grew into nuance and complication with every new space it entered, creolizing and matching local tastes and available foods. Taro for dasheen for bhaji. White bread to hold the curry of bunny chow. Daal puri and bust-up-shot/shirt. It makes sense to my own poetic mind that the meeting of these various writers can be held in the karahee, as I see it, put together to produce something new, something nourishing, something complicated and ancestral, something constantly evolving. What this something is, is how we survive our histories of forced labor, how our ancestors reach toward us, and how we, as writers, either reach back or reach away.

There have been few collections of creative writing from the Coolie Labor Diaspora, and those that are collected often function as comparison of language, concerns, and expressed and received "Indiannesses," created and maintained locally in the diasporic spaces. Before launching into the brilliance of these assembled writers and the new mehfil they create in these pages, I must be clear about what exactly I mean by Coolie Labor Diaspora—why use this incendiary word to create and reify community bonds from disparate communities across the globe. What connects this particular constellation of writers is precisely this: a colonial-era inheritance of trafficking and labor. The term *Coolie* was given to the indentured laborers who the British kidnapped, lured, and tricked into replacing the cheap labor of enslaved Africans and indigenous populations of the places where their extractive colonies fruited sugar cane, rice, and other goods for global exchange. The coffers that were lined from this exploitation—by what David Dabydeen terms "a reinvention of slavery"—still keep the wealth and jewels purloined from *les damnés de la terre.*

The period of Indian indenture (India under the British Raj and not the India of today's geopolitical borders) lasted officially from 1838 to 1917, but in practice, it began sooner and ended later (according to Ballengee, the period of indenture extended from the 1820s to the 1920s). As a poet and writer myself, I often wonder if this period ever ended, whether indenture has left its white scars on the bodies of the inheritors of indenture so much that our various communities remained plagued by the fallout of Empire: language attrition, misogyny, homophobia, racism, alcoholism and substance abuse, and diabetes—just to name a few of the demons. Whether or not these rakshasas, pretas, or jinns appear explicitly in the writing varies, as you, reader, will experience. The mere haunting of these things, indeed the hauntings from the cane field, ghosts the outlooks and sensibilities of our various worlds. This is not to say that we are still bound people without agency to create and evolve cultural practices—this is to say instead that we are taking the steerage of our courses instead of depending on some unnamed imperial patron.

And this brings me to why the word *Coolie.* There has been much work done by writers and thinkers (like Rajkumari Singh, e.g., who wrote the polemic "I Am a Coolie") to use this word as one of empowerment, one that can be reclaimed and harnessed for its specificity and its power. The poet and cultural theorist Khal Torabully, in his cowritten book with Maria Carter, illuminates the concept of a Coolie becoming through his ideas around Coolitude: configuring the Coolie Labor Diaspora, its histories, and its literature. Christopher Ballengee in *Global Studies South* describes this concept as "framework for remembering dislocation." He says,

> As a creative practice, coolitude draws on traumatic memories of the past to inform post-indenture identities, importantly referencing the centrality of creolization and cultural mixing in present-day notions of self and community. As an analytical perspective, a coolitudian approach moreover provides poetic

> context that informs histories of indenture and post-indenture along creolized trajectories in multicultural, postcolonial societies.[1]

I use this word personally because it evinces this particular history: a word that used to have an anti-racialized velocity but, wielded by imperialists, drove the people it sought to locate into racialized competition with Black and Indigenous people across the colonies. It is in this spellcasting that includes a rigorous backward glance that I predict a new, queerer version of community that reclaims the potential of this appellation—the word *Coolie* as descriptive of labor and relationship to Empire instead of referring specifically to India, the subcontinent, or other Asian countries (such as Java and China) that suffered this brand of dehumanization, a different species of Césaire's *thingification*. For me, this word summons cane fields, razor-sharp leaves, survival despite the neglect of our masters.

There is a futurity to the term *Coolie* or even *Qoolie* (the "Q" here functioning, as Ryan Persadie writes, to locate the queer protentional of this word through the act of Derridian différance meaning delayed and deferred until beholding the written word, a metaphor for the queer in plain sight yet invisibilized[2]), since about this term Torabully and Carter write,

> For many years, however, "coolie" was a symbol of economic degradation and social submissiveness, and the descendants of coolies felt themselves to be equally stigmatized, exoticized and ostracized. The reclamation of the "coolie" and the transformation of the indenture heritage is an ongoing process.[3]

It is in service to this ongoing process that I take this term and claim it as my own. As a writer, custodian of history, and editor, I, myself, am ever-evolving. Yet in a more personal way, I turn this word toward my own first person, tenderly holding the beauty of my mother, my Ayah, my Aji, my father, my Nana, and my Aja, while I call out to them through my writing. When my sister and I, now in North America, talk about meeting South Asian people, we speak in familiar terms.

After attending a party hosted by one of her queer friends, my sister called me on the phone.

"Raim," she uses her name for me—my call name—"I just met a gay guy named Dinesh, and I think you would love him." My sister, ever my wingman.

"Is he Desi or Coolie?" I ask.

"Dinesh a one Coolie bai," she responds in Guyanese Creole.

This exchange is common for us, and it is a subtle yet powerful illumination of our South Asian diasporic dynamics. Desi is a word for immigrants and their children, more recently from India than our community is. Coolie is powerful; it proves an intimate connection of history and potential connections along those lines.

This special issue of *Mānoa* represents new writing from established and emerging voices from this particular diaspora, one that I am intimately tied to through my history and through the spirits that haunt me still. The British took Indians from the depots in the then ports of Calcutta and Madras in repurposed slave ships to their settlements and colonies in Fiji, Mauritius, Reunion, South Africa, Jamaica, Trinidad, Guyana, and Surinam. This issue includes writers from these various sites and plantation communities who have Creolized and changed through staying past their indenture contracts. Several generations after this settling by ancestors who were coolies bound to Empire, these writers and artists practice. This issue of writing from the Coolie Diaspora asks: *what is the inheritance of the cane field, the cane-sap residue marking the descendants of this system of indenture?*

When approaching the writers to send their work for consideration, I wanted to highlight voices that were emerging and less well known in the field of Coolie Labor Diasporic studies, a field that has become trendy in recent years for people outside of the communities studied to build their careers on Coolie labor, still. We are more than those authors typically studied and overrepresented by academics still caught up on Kalapani Poetics, who do not read writing from the Coolie Labor Diaspora past the 1990s. I am not interested here, and neither are the writers only concerned with cultural holdovers and narratives of crossing the ocean. Our ancestors crossed long, long ago. Generations grew and fell. The writers assembled in this karahee, this mehfil of flavors, ask, *what now?*

Punctuating the issue are the images from Andil Gosine's sequence called "Offerings," in which the artist presents images of the items that he offered to the ocean—that veritable god of migration—that set the tone for how readers enter and interact with the writing. These images move from object to object, insisting on the remembering of diasporic situatedness and the ways our various offerings have changed. Andre Bagoo's poem "The Inheritance: A Sequence" plays with memory—the trick of erasure, reinterpretation, and re-reinterpretations the speaker uses to make sense of the poem—and even the world. The poets Sudesh Mishra, Shivanee Ramlochan, C. Govender, Will Depoo, Chandanie Somwaru, Nicholas Augustus Peters, Gitan Djeli, and Francine Simon use their various local positionings to evidence their inheritance of labor and the forward look toward the future of their own lives that are context-specific while recalling, however vaguely, a Coolie inheritance.

I am excited that this issue also includes girmitiya[4] songs from Fiji translated by Alisha Prasad from Hindi/Bhojpuri as well as songs from Tamil via Mauritius translated by Ari Gautier. Original songs from the international musician Raj Mohan, written originally in Sarnami Bhojpuri and translated into English, read as poems, coupled with new translations of Mauritius's Ananda Devi, make this issue one whose breadth spans the emerging to the established with breathtaking depth. Still, writers like Kevin Jared Hosein, Nadia Misir, and Jay Aja provide the clear inheritances of colonial dispossession: violence, poverty, trauma, and ecological crises, all while highlighting the act of survival as anti-imperialist.

I also include my own translations of, in my mind, important Indo-Caribbean music that I have been thinking through, including a ghazal and another song-text-read-as-poem in Urdu. The issue ends with a poem written by writer and poet Vinod Busjeet, who recasts his visit to Trinidad. A kind of Global South to Global South conversation. Originally from Mauritius, the poem's speaker's familiarity with Coolie culture from the Caribbean is routed through the touchstone of Nobel Prize winner V. S. Naipaul, a writer beloved and reviled for his ideas of coloniality, Indianness, and Caribbean cultural productions. In the poem's speaker's beholding of others from the Coolie Diaspora, readers come away with the ideas of how, despite distance and divergent histories, we are connected through the experience of becoming *Coolie*, of the plantation. Of the cane-sap that still traumatizes us while delighting us.

There are so many writers and artists that I wish I could have included in this very special issue, including Aliyah Khan, Vidyaratha Kissoon, Kelly Sinnapah Mary, Ingrid Persaud, Subraj Singh, Jessica Nirvana Ram, Divya Persaud, Ian Harnarine, Nadia Bourne, Anu Lakhan, Naben Ruthnum, and so many more. I hope to think of our communities as expansive and dynamic, changing through time with the potential to create alliances with the folks that we encounter. When I lived in Hawaiʻi as a graduate student from 2013 to 2017, I was struck by the cultural similarities of my own Caribbean inheritance, my own familial pidgin, our own sugar traumas, and our own erasure of Indigenous and Black peoples in favor of national unity. It is my sincerest hope that this issue and these voices resonate with those that call out from the ʻāina, those voices struggling and rejoicing toward Kānaka Maoli sovereignty. I hope that the resonances in these pages harmonize with the joys and heartbreaks of a kingdom overthrown.

I envision *Karahee from the Cane Fields: Writing from the Coolie Diaspora* as a cultural meeting place for a literary reconvening of those who are haunted by ancestors who suffered the punishment of the Empire's extracted labor. The karahee here is the issue itself; the writings are various foods to be cooked together on a chulha, or if in diaspora the earth stove is unavailable, then cooked on a makeshift fireside of cement blocks and whatever wood we can find. What is evident in these pages for you, reader, to discover, marvel at, and be astounded by is our survival and tenacity—that despite our destitutions and our impoverishments, we still grow tall and we still bend toward the light.

NOTES

1. Ballengee, Christopher. "Coolitude." *Global South Studies, U.Va.* https://globalsouthstudies.as.virginia.edu/key-concepts/coolitude (accessed December 22, 2023).
2. Persadie, Ryan. "'Meh Just Realize I's Ah Coolie Bai': Indo-Caribbean Masculinities, Chutney Genealogies, and Qoolie Subjectivities." *Middle Atlantic Review of Latin American Studies*, vol. 4, no. 2, 2020, pp. 56–86.
3. Carter, Marina, and Khal. *Coolitude: An Anthology of the Indian Labour Diaspora*. London: Anthem, 2002.
4. An Indian indentured laborer, the word derives from the émigrés pronunciation of "agreement" in English to "girmit." The addition of the "-iya" suffix makes the word mean "those of the agreement."

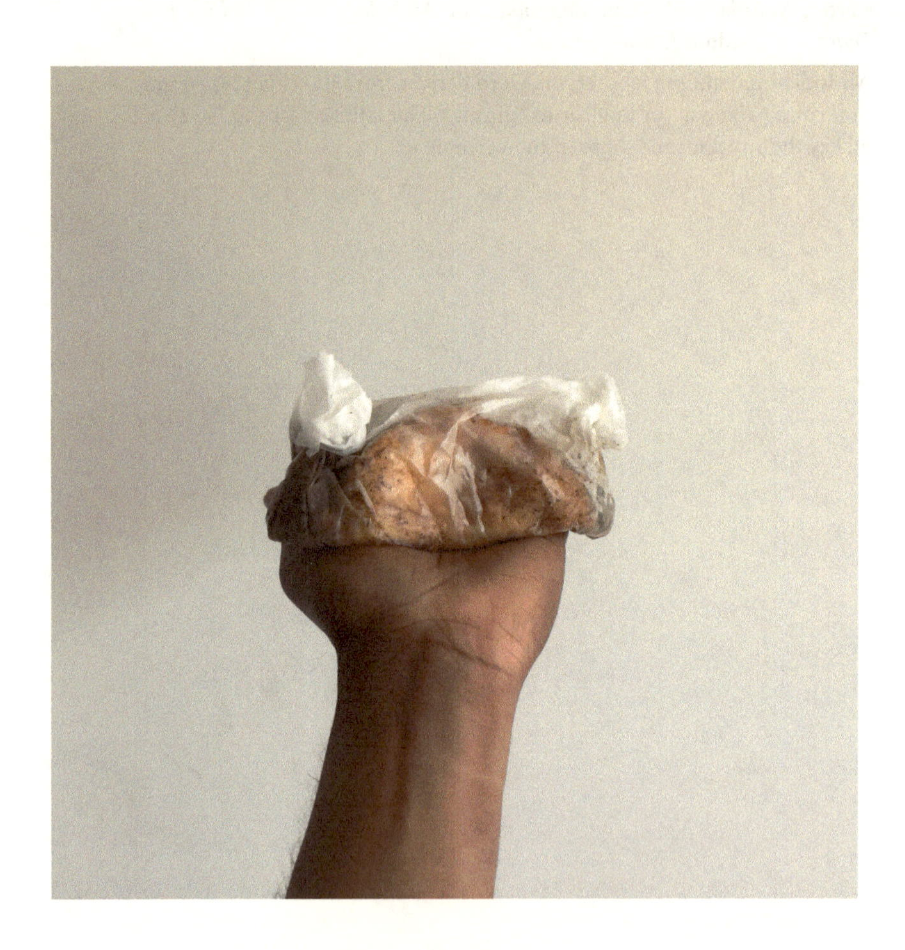

Photograph by Andil Gosine

ANDIL GOSINE

Offerings: Artist Statement

Soon as I reach a sea, the call is visceral, automatic—I have to offer her a flower. At Mayaro, the Atlantic coastal beach in Trinidad that I most frequented as a child, that was the first thing that would happen on every visit. Before the fire was set up to cook a curry duck, before the caps of Carib came off, and before the sandcastles were built, my grandmother and I scoured the landscape for flowers, of which there were not many. All the women performed this act, as did the occasional grown man. But all the children learned to follow our aunties, mothers, and grandmothers: clasp a flower and offer it to Ganga, mother of the sea. Thank her for her care and nourishment; wonder at her force.

My favourite Hindu rituals shared this element of an offering. At pujas, we offered food to the fire and to Mother Earth before jhandis were hoisted to her. At temple, flowers were offered to the murtis of gods and goddesses, and the glow of deeyas' light was offered to our elders.

Echoes of this past were present in the first of the offerings I photographed, of ixoras in hand offered to the sea. In this diptych, bright pink ixoras were held in one hand, and a finished necklace of them—the kind I made as a child—were in the second photograph. In the exhibition of them, the images were placed next to a pink pair of boxers of a lover, my name embroidered over their French branding.

These tensions, in which the weights of past formations structure present feelings of exile and home and which have transformed "home" from a material world to a space in my psyche, inhabit the images that followed.

The material worlds are still powerful prompts, though. I was in a West Indian grocer's store in Brooklyn when it occurred to me to photograph that block of New Zealand cheddar that every Trinidadian expatriate covets. Then came the zaboca. I walked down to get doubles from A&A's and, of course, had to do that one too, along with the pepper sauce that came on the side for my roti. I received these goods as offerings, and something about their capture in photography provided my gratitude for the companionship and comfort they brought me. As I shot more and more offerings—the nine pictured here are just a sample—I felt it would be dishonest to confine the objects to just those that had Caribbean traces. I think I was imagining this collection as a kind of bundle, like those brought by indentures, but the great thing about creole space is the impossibility of containing culture. So I added items that stamped the trail of my personal experiences as well: the bandage covering up my blood test, a catalog from an art exhibition curated by Hilton Als, and gifts from my first (the ceramic of Spanish architecture) and latest (the pink ring) dalliances. Finally, in this little group of nine, is the hand of my aunt Droopathie in mine. When the project is complete (and there's something particularly creole about my unawareness of how far away I am from completion), there will be 108 "offerings." The number is another unyielding holdover from my Hindu upbringing (during meditation we chanted "Om Namah Shivaya" 108 times), all of them evidence of exchanges that mark the search, negotiation and claim of home in the dark waters of exile.

ANDRE BAGOO

The Inheritance: A Sequence

THE INHERITANCE

If I have no children I will adopt
my parents as my own.
In our family
the children die before their elders
who are not concerned with generations.
The parents forget their forefathers'
names, but remember their skin color.
They dream
of fair complexions and large houses
and yards to store old refrigerators.
They sleep on beds not meant for sharing.
They pray for a better tomorrow.
Occasionally, they have dreams of death.
Their children have none.
They know nothing of pleasure.
They work to keep what they borrow
to keep those who kept them.
Until they are released
from the safety of houses,
and find the dedolent sky will not do
for tomorrow is really yesterday.
In our family
parents live inside their elders
and elders live inside their children
and no one can tear the generations apart.

I

have

names

for

the

sky

THE CANE INHERIT

if I rewrite my poem
I will

rename this color
what does
it mean to rewrite something
you never wrote?
for sharing
for a better tomorrow

to keep
to
release
I was never safe in houses

tear the generations apart

THE RIT E

if you have no children
you are fucked, a
nobody
for all of life is solely
concerned with generations
and their generation
for we
dream
of generations
and the children must be protected
they are meant to generate
we are meant to generate
all who generate are successful generators

(say nothing of
they work to keep generating
they cannot attend your dinner because they are generating
they cannot reply to your text because they are generating
they don’t get out of the house much, as a mom
you are killed because they are generating
how busy they are generating
until they are released,
they will be generators of generations, excuse them,
do
for tomorrow is really yesterday

what a success you are

HER

if the cancer comes back
there is nothing I can do

it is always someone else's turn
what a success I am

living among the
architecture of forgetting

                but flesh is an archive
                        of her voice
                        of freshly baked bread
                        the touch of her hand

                        trapped
                                in

    tomorrow   yesterday.

Mother, nothing can tear us apart

HE

h e h e

he h e he
h e h e
he he fore
skin
he
large

bed
he
he h e
he
he pleasure
he he
he he
release
he h e he
he
for tomorrow is really

inside him

the one
I knew before

yes, it comes back
the cancer
the poem
the wars

when I told you, you said I imagined it
the slavery
the indenture
the colonialism
the genocide
the neo-colonialism
the cutting of my
                                        tongue
the Earth being given to you –
I imagined it, you said
this was all given to you in a dream, you said
in a dream you possessed it, you said
all the flowers are mine, you said
the wildflowers, you said
the blue flowers, you said
the flowers yet to flower, you said
my tears are worth more than yours, you said,
as you take back what you already took long ago
from me

how does one end a poem?

ON WRITING "THE INHERITANCE"

There was a boy on the swim team who would beat me up. I liked it.

I wasn't on the swim team, but I would see him at P.E. I hated P.E. I'd sit with the other geeks in the stands. He would hang out with his teammates at the edge of the pool, and they'd strip, shower, then do laps. I'd watch him, and he'd watch me. For a very long time, that's how things went. But one day, I made the mistake of going to use the urinal in the locker room at the back of the stands. He followed me. He whistled as he opened his locker and took out his kit. As I washed my hands, I saw him in the mirror. He stripped off his wet speedos, dried himself, and put on white cotton briefs. When he saw me looking at him, he came over, shoved me against the wall, and punched me. I buckled over. He grabbed my head and rubbed my face against his crotch. He said nothing. I said nothing. He left. I left. I walked home alone through the Savannah. Yellow butterflies swarmed in the mid-afternoon heat.

Next P.E. class, I avoided the locker room. But he still stared at me and followed me with his eyes. I was taking a shortcut home one day, cutting through the middle of the Savannah, when I realized he was behind me. It was that weird time in the day long after the morning wave of joggers, yet still too early for the evening one. In the center of the park, nobody was around. It was as though we were in the middle of a still, green sea. No one would hear me scream if I tried. But I didn't. He tackled me to the ground so fast that I didn't have time to react. Or I didn't want to react. I yielded to him, his weight, his force, and his hate. Above me was the stifling sun, the warmth of his body, and his hot breaths against my neck. Below me, the heat of the soil. He placed my neck in a choke hold. All I could think of was the smell: the smell of fresh grass, of sweat, of earthwarm. And then he let me go. He got up. He spit on my face and left. I got hard.

History is an erasure poem, in which no matter how much you distort the original text, something—a shape, a spirit, a presence in absence—remains. Silence can be a lament. It can also be a memorial. I've never written about this guy before. Maybe queerness is the inheritance of silence. I'm so ashamed, I don't even want to tell you his name. He's married now and has kids. I've checked. Yet here he is. Here, he always was, a beast creeping around in my poems, in my essays, and in my stories, a presence stalking me through his absence.

***

In the white space of the page, I still see him, even if my readers don't, standing naked in the locker room, with the fleshy vulnerability of his tip, the cruelty of his dark brown eyes, and the perfect carving of his torso, naked and ablaze. I can feel his embrace, expressed first in violence, in the stifling power of muscles, in his wish to contain me, to contain himself, and then, through his embrace of himself, to express, somehow, a desire.

What we think of as beautiful is inherited, isn't it? Inherited from decades of programming, inherited from our own experience. This guy became a standard against which I would measure all others—my Shiva, my Olokun, my Apollo—you name the god. But it is possible that nothing informs my view of him—that I found him beautiful because I found him beautiful and terrifying.

My poem "The Inheritance" came of its own accord. Or did I inherit it? Do we write poems, or do we inherit them? Maybe I invented the poem. Maybe I inherited the possibility of inventing it. I said to myself: take one poem you have already published and erase it. History is an erasure poem.

But what happens when the poem goes a little haywire and you begin to deviate from the deviation? When constraint cannot help but turn to freedom, the way the body will always seek what it really wants?

Sometimes, when I write poems, I invent things. And sometimes, when I invent things, they come true. By this, I mean there are times when I have written things in a poem that have never happened to me before. And then, a few weeks later, they happen. In a poem, a black cat appears. And suddenly, my yard is filled with black cats. In a poem, I go for drinks with an old friend. A few weeks later, they come to town.

And then there are the times when I don't know what has happened to me until I write about what has happened to me, and the poem is like doing the work of archaeology, brushing away layers of time to unearth relics that have been buried: a cup, a vase, the archaic torso of a man, who may or may not have existed, but who exists now in a new, eternal present. No one can tear us apart.

Photograph by Andil Gosine

Sugarcane

Was it an openness that made us swim
Breaststroke through the cane-reeds? I remember
The sky, endless, above the spiked current.
We'd no purpose which was purpose enough
To wade out of the green roar, lance in hand.
How, on the curbside, we rat-stripped the bark
Till bared, it grew moon-bright and syrupy.
I loved most the tensed jaw, the gummy hands,
The spat-out spongy joy of the grownup.
I can't say who was the first to cast out
The hoarded bagasse of all our boyhood.
Do you go, as I do, down the growth-rings
Of some sweet sea-tormented memory,
But remember no longer how to swim?

The Milky Way in a Bag

I was six when Father gave me a star
Screwdriver and pointed to the night-sky.
The clouds, sheepish, had quit with the sun.
I unscrewed the Centaur and the Crater.
Next I drew out the Dipper and the Dog.
The gold studs of the Hunter I plundered
And loosened the guts on the Lyre for fun.
Punching holes in the keel of the Argo,
I caught the fish by its fin, but squandered
The chance to bald the Eagle. By and by,
As the sky grew darker, I gleaned a swag
Of winking asterisks and, by night's end,
The whole of Milky Way was in the bag.
Now undo, said he, the work of your hand.

The Spinning Top

You few, companions of my boyhood,[1]
Do you recall the spinning top
We wound from the beak upwards
And let rip under the raintree?
What spun then, the top or us?
Whirling dervishes lost inside the whirl?
How mindful were we of mother's call,
The fast-thinning schoolyard,
The struck gong of the plunging sun?
I can no longer remember (can you?)
When our spent top toppled over
And we went, forever, our separate ways.

[1] The poem's first line is an allusion to Rilke's *Sonnets to Orpheus*, and in particular Sonnet 8, Part 2, which I read as an elegy to childhood.

Gulli-Danda

Cut from a broomstick that had lost its spell,
The gulli was shorter than the danda
By four lengths and tapered at either end.
We laid it across a shallow pit dug
For that purpose and I, coming up heads,
Lofted it up over your lunging hand
With the tapered point of the longer stick
Before laying a bridge over the void.
When the bird of your gulli missed its mark,
I hit down on its beak to make it fly
Then cracked it up in mid-flight to drive it
Far away from the pit of foreshadows.
By the time you counted up the stick-yards
I'd plundered from you, I was grownup, gone.

The Boys from Bruegel

I can't dredge up the kid-made rules, can you?
When we thumb-shot the buoyed up taws, was I
Upstanding or on my haunches? Did you
Knuckle down in the backyard, your finger
Sprung back like a tensed asp as you sized up
The cunt-rift? What sank in first: my aggie
Or your scottie? Who first bagged the keepsie
And felt the clunk of delight in his shorts?
Others, too, were there: the wily cupid
Who never wagered his rounded lapis
And yet ravened greedily on our envy.
Were we forever the boys from Bruegel
Huddled together to witness ourselves
Counting the lost craters of a childhood?

Harappa

We found them on the patio one morning,
The terracotta toys, in a boxful
Of riparian sand. A bird on the wing
Came flapping down on a sill, then a bull
Thick-necked, twig-horned, went bellowing into
The yard. Who was fonder of the wheeled ram
Because it had no free will, me or you?
And was the lamb truly bleating "I am"
Or did we dream it up in the one dream
Of childhood? We stole from each its slumber
To awaken for ourselves a summer
Interred for centuries inside our gene.
We had seals, a great bath, beads of amber,
An ekka trotting up to Harappa.

ANONYMOUS

Girmitiya Song from Fiji

TRANSLATED BY ALISHA PRASAD

This song is a selection from my designed art book, *Yaad Karo*. In the publication, I use significant objects from the Indo-Fijian indenture period as a method to introduce to the reader stories from my ancestors that highlight their journey over the *kala pani* (black water), their lives on the plantation and what got them through the exhausting labour required of them. The publication is made up of poems, folksongs, book excerpts, and archival imagery, along with my own writing, drawings, objects, family photographs, and more.

In *Yaad Karo*, it was important to feature folksongs and poems that have been passed down orally through generations by my ancestors and other *Girmitiyas* (Fiji Hindi word for indentured labourers brought from India to Fiji by British colonial forces) to highlight my personal connection to the project as well as bring light to the voices and unheard stories from indentured labour. I chose the folksong/poem based on which significant object was being explored in the publication. In *Yaad Karo*, the folksongs and poems are also featured alongside my own drawings of my memories of Fiji and how I envisioned my ancestors' histories. This is how I "disrupted" the use of colonial images, which didn't capture the warmth, personality, or individuality of the person being photographed. The images felt cold and harsh, as they were only taken for mostly colonial business records.

Out of the selected collection of folksongs and poems, I translated "Woh che aur aat foot ka CSR kamra" from English into Fiji Hindi. When translating this song, I aimed to convey the depth of emotion and storytelling of my Girmitiya ancestors, to have it sound as if we were hearing it from their mouths in our mother tongue.

WOH CHE AUR AAT FOOT KA CSR KAMRA

Woh che aur aat foot ka CSR karma
Humare sukh ka sahara tha
Oosme hum apna upkaaran aur koodari
Aur jata aur choola
Usme khana pakane ka lakri
Humaar mahal
Jisme banaye hai hum apne sona ka deewaar

THE SIX FOOT BY EIGHT FOOT CSR ROOM[1]

The six foot by eight foot CSR room
Is the source of all comfort for us.
In it, we keep our tools and hoe,
And also the grinding stone and the hearth.
In it is also kept the firewood.
It is our single- and double-story palace,
In which is made our golden parapet.

---

[1]Brij Lal, *Song from Fiji in Chalo Jahaji: On a Journey through Indenture in Fiji*, 2000.

ARI GAUTIER

Cane Sap, Drops of Blood, Beads of Sweat

TRANSLATED BY AJITH KANNA

"Pāzha pônè maschettou," I will never get used to it.

Nothing beats our koduvakatthi. Panchami drops the machete and takes the end of her sari to wrap the injured finger. A few drops of blood mixed with cane sap fall onto the hot ground. The red sun at its zenith is merciless. The young woman wipes away the beads of sweat running down her neck. Cane sap, drops of blood, beads of sweat—her life on the plantation is far from being dry.

***

"You have blood here," Nagamootoo plants a kiss on the neck, marked by the red marks left by the bloody mundanai. He runs his tongue over his lips without letting her go and finds himself enjoying the salty, metallic taste of blood, sweat, and sugar cane sap.

"Mmmm... it tastes like urukka," he closes his eyes to remember the taste of the condiment.

"Make something to eat while I take a bath. My belly, it shouts."

Feigning anger, Panchami pushes him away and takes the path towards the Ravine de Saint Gilles. Astonished to hear her speak Creole, Nagamootoo smiles and leaves towards the kitchen. The absence of his beloved suits him because he had decided to prepare a real feast for her this evening. Panchami's thoughts escape following the Bruniquel Canal. She was only sixteen or seventeen years old when she followed her husband Veeraswamy to settle in Reunion Island. After his second contract, the latter returned to Pondicherry to find a wife, and it was quite natural that he married his niece Panchami. She never imagined that her life would take such a turn. Going far from her family to an unknown destination scared her. But these distant lands were not foreign to her, for she lived in Coolietheruvu, which was near the temple of Draupadi at the entrance to the village of Murungapakkam, south of Pondicherry. Called this way because of the inhabitants who had a connection with people leaving for the sugarcane islands, the coolie street lived to the rhythm of the departures and returns of indentured laborers who immutably defied their destiny. Panchami was a young girl dressed in paavadai-sattai when Veeraswamy first returned from Maurise theevu. His robust body and big mustache used to scare her. She hid behind her mother every time he was looking to attract her to him, to have fun with her. She observed him from the corner of her eye without daring to approach him. She never felt close to him, despite her family's jokes, because she was Veeraswamy's bride. Her destiny dressed in daawani, who awaited his return, left draped in sari towards La Reunion.

***

Panchami abandons her memories for a moment at the entrance of the first tunnel dug into the rock. One has to be careful because the slope of the ravine is steep, probably due to a scree. She crosses the second tunnel, then a narrow gap, and finally arrives at Bassin Malheur. Tired from walking, she sits on a rock at the foot of the waterfall.

"Pāzha pônè Mascareignes!" Tears flow when she thinks of the ship that transported this cursed disease, which took away her Veeraswamy. She was angry with Captain Joseph d'Agnel and his supercargo Joseph Menon who disdained the cholera that was raging in Kilwa, from where the ship left loaded with African indentured laborers. She had prayed to all the gods and had walked miles and miles to go to the new chapel of La Salette in Saint-Leu to save her husband. Being Hindu, this dual religious practice was not foreign to her because, for generations, her family had frequently gone to the church of Our Lady of Health of Ariyankuppam. But fate decided otherwise. Veeraswamy succumbed to illness and left her alone without a family. Panchami's first instinct was to return home, but knowing the fate reserved for widows in Indian society, she dismissed this idea. They would have dressed her in white, confined her in four walls without any social life, and at the age of twenty, her existence would have ended without tasting the pleasures of life. Panchami did not want to comply with this unjust tradition, so she decided to stay in La Reunion and continue the life she had started. Come what may!

***

"Néna rien ke ton dent ke lé blan kom un grain de riz," Nagamootoo hands the plate to Panchami who was enjoying her favorite rum. "You outdid yourself today, my gâté! It's a real feast that you prepared for me there."

"Riz sosso, cari de sauté de porc, rougail saucisses au piment oiseau and rougail boucané bringel," a melancholic sillarai pāttu rises towards the misty sky to interrupt the sad silence of the plantation.

"I feel good in your arms." Curled up against Nagamootoo, Panchami draws insignificant shapes on his chest.

"Then why don't you stay with me, Panchami?" His voice becomes pleading.

"Don't spoil this pleasant moment, Nagamootoo. She, like you, is also part of my life. I can not choose."

***

Panchami hurries on; she is late for the big day. They were going to open the Massalin Karly Koilu, which was the first temple on the plantation, and everyone was excited. Panchami finished her day earlier than usual and went to bathe at Bassin Malheur, her favorite spot. On her way back, she is still overcome by doubt. Should she go withRaharianne or Nagamootoo? The latter would have been the natural choice given that he was a Hindu like her, but Panchami was not afraid of the ladilafé. Everyone knew she was a liberated woman. A smell of suruttu greets her when she crosses the edge of the sugar cane field. No doubt, it's Moothianpillay! Disturbed by his presence, she tries to avoid him, but the man gets in her way and prevents her from moving further. He's been lurking around her for a while. His lustful gaze had followed her from a distance since the first day of her arrival on the island.

***

But since Veeraswamy's disappearance, Moothianpillay was no longer hiding. He often came to bother her. The man did not seem to give up his advances despite Panchami's multiple refusals.

"This is not the time, Moothianpillay, I am in a hurry."

"You have time for the whole world, but never for me," he said mockingly. His cheerful voice irritates Panchami, who tries to get around him.

"I am not in the mood to joke. What do you finally want from me? Be reasonable, you know very well that I am not alone."

"Exactly! Why refuse me when you have more than one person in your bed?"

"What I do in my bed is my business. I sleep with who I want and how I want. It is not your problem."

"That you are sleeping with Nagamootoo is one thing, but sharing your bed with that filthy slut is disgusting! Am I less than a slave?"

"I will not allow you to talk about Raharianne that way! I do what I want, no one has the right to judge me. Especially not you, Moothianpillay!" Panchami tries to push him with all her strength to force her way through, but the man is strong. He grabs Panchami's hand and twists her arm behind her back.

"Let me go, you brute, otherwise I will stir up the neighbours."

"You can shout as much as you want, my dear, there is no one left. They all went to the koilu."

Panchami understands at this moment that she is really in danger. The scoundrel had well-premeditated his crime. The sound of thappattai echoes in the distance; the ceremony has just started. There is no chance that anyone will come to her rescue. The smell of Moothianpillay's putrid breath disgusts her. She feels his hard cock swollen with bestial desire when he holds her to him. Panchami chokes. She breaks free from his hold and claws at his face.

"Thevudia mundai!" Moothianpillay rushes at her and slaps her several times until she falls to the ground. "You depraved thing! Sleeping with a man is not enough for you, do you also need a woman? What do you have between your legs, you bitch? Come on, I will satisfy you for good!"

Moothianpillay looks around. Panchami takes advantage of this moment to get up and run home. The man runs behind her with a long stick of sugar cane. She barely has time to get into the kitchen when Moothianpillay joins her and grabs her by the hair. He flips her onto the floor, lies down full length on her, and spreads her thighs with his legs. With his left hand, he holds her arms, while with his right hand, he tries to push the sugar cane stick inside the young woman. Panchami screams and struggles. Moothianpillay lets go of her arms and puts his hand over her mouth to muffle the screams. Panchami's hands are groping and searching for something. The pace of thappattai is more and more frantic, and Karly is coming out of the koilu for the procession. In a final gesture of despair, Panchami grabbed what she was looking for.

Moothianpillay's headless body lies on the ground.

Pāzha pônè maschettou!

Cane Sap, drops of blood, beads of sweat.

ARI GAUTIER

Transoceanic Destiny of a Sillarai Pāttu: A Lyric Experiment

TRANSLATED BY AJITH KANNA

Mannum poyidichu, ponnum poyidichu
Nilamum poyidichu, valamum poyidichu
Nilavum teyindu poyidichu, pagalum teyindu poyidichu
Utraar uravinar illamal, nadu kadalil tavikiromai.

We lost our land, we lost our property
We lost our fields, we lost our resources
The moon has eclipsed and the day has darkened
Without those around us, we sink into this ocean.

Marimootoo's eyes were as dry as the soil that had nourished him and his family for centuries. The cracked earth looked like his broken heart. What to do? Where to go? This unprecedented famine had chased him from his village. This disaster was a real curse! He was the first to inherit this field. His ancestors, who were working as serfs for the Zamindar of the region, have never had the happiness of owning the slightest piece of land. This good fortune had become his misfortune. Looking for a solution, he had wandered for days in this unknown city that was Pondicherry. Destiny pushed him towards a Mestry who promised him a better life. He did not even know his destination. One needs to know how to read first. The dark sea was going to write a destiny that his blue thumb had placed on the document.

Maurise theevu, he was told when he boarded. His thoughts brought him back to his children to whom he had promised to return at the next moon. And this moon was waning as the days vanished. Without family and without friends, the ship's slipway has become hell. The sea was engulfing the hope of seeing his native land and his family.

Naadum illai, kaadum illai
Maramum Illai, nizhalum illai
Thottamum illai, thuravum illai
Naadodi pôl alaiguiromai.

Without country, without timberland
Without trees, without shadows
Without grove, without water
We wander like nomads.

Despite the lamentations that rose from the boat bunker, Rukmini displayed a delightful smile. She knew that Govind would appear at any moment. Her whole day was punctuated by the hope and desire to meet him. This furtive meeting on the ship deck at nightfall was her only satisfaction in this monotonous crossing. Since their gazes met at the port of Pondicherry, her life had become a stormy sea. Only his presence could calm these waves of love that invaded her heart. He was the only one who could give her some semblance of comfort in her tumultuous life. Married and widowed at a very young age, her life has turned into unprecedented misery. She had escaped the pyres, but her existence was purgatory. Stripped of her social and family rights, Rukmini languished among her in-laws, who accused her of the death of their son. Not wanting to feed a useless mouth, they planned to get rid of her by sending her to an ashram to live a reclusive life. But everyone knew that these places were more places of pleasure for upper-caste men than spiritual retreats. Rukmini did not want to end her days as a prostitute. Also, she had fled her native place of Bihar and found herself in Kalkutta to try a new life. Destiny pushed her to Chandernagore, where she learned that a boat was leaving Pondicherry towards an unknown destination. On this calm night, the two lovers were enjoying the Choorah that Rukmini had carefully kept in a dented bowl. They dreamed of a new life and a new land where their forbidden love could germinate without social constraints. A cloud passed and hid the mischievous moon. The waves were silent for a moment.

"I love you," whispered Govind. La Grande Soufrière appeared on the horizon as the moon reappeared.

Engai pogirôm, edarku pogirôm
Eppozhudu thirumbi varuvôm
Endrukkuda theriammal
Inda paavi kappalil talladuguiromai.

Where are we going? For what are we going?
Without knowing our return
Our destiny is swaying on this cursed boat.

Samikannu had difficulty getting to sleep. His body, aching from the backbreaking work, was demanding rest. His head, still invaded by the Sillarai Pāttu composed on board, refused to die in the face of the songs of locusts coming from the fields of sugarcane. Had he known this work would be so tiring, he would never have left his native country to come to this foreign land. Even if it meant starving.

Pampered and spoiled by his parents despite their poverty, the young boy was never concerned about his future. His life would have been completely different if this cursed cyclone had not taken everything away on its way. The house and their modest shop were taken away by the water. Having never learned his family's hereditary trade of shoemaker, Samikannu did not know what to do. Bewildered, he went to seek help from family in Pondicherry. Welcoming and kind at first, his uncle, after a few months, made him understand that the young boy had to fend for himself. Samikannu's fate was cast on the nebulous road of uncertainty. In the port of Madras, he tied his future to the masts of the Elbe and let the wind decide his destiny. Indonesia, Papua New Guinea, Australia, two months later, he set his feet in Fiji.

Tears of joy flowed down her cheeks, pierced by the Vel. His first Kaavadi! He had lived on the main island of Viti Levu for years. Rocked by the calm waters of the Nadi River, his life had taken a normal course. From being hired, he had become a free worker and had started his own business. His wife and three children lived in perfect happiness. When Ramasami Pillai shared his dream of building a Murugan temple, Samikannu had dedicated his body and soul to ensure that the project was successful. When the temple bell rang for the first time, he felt immense joy. The culmination of a life. Through his cheeks, the Vel was the symbol of a successful life. He, the outcast to whom temples were closed in his homeland! He put the Kaavadi on his shoulders and danced cheerfully the Kaavadi Aattam to the rhythm of Thappu!

Nagappan ended his story. His wet eyes blurred in front of the screen of his computer, where he had just finished writing the life of his ancestor.

ANANDA DEVI

Five Selections from Danser sur tes braises

TRANSLATED BY KAZIM ALI

When I began translating Ananda Devi's last book of poetry, *When the Night Agrees to Speak to Me (Quand la nuit consent à me parler)*, I was in francophone India, and when I completed the first draft, I was on the shore of the Indian Ocean, across wide expanses from Mauritius, where Devi had been raised. Her mother tongue is Telugu, but it is lost to her. We share this: migrants who crossed many borders in our lives, spoke many languages, but not our mother tongues. As much an affinity as that was, I was translating across gender, across culture, across generations, indeed across languages. Something about rendering the poems of that book—honest in a way that seared me, angry in a way I had not yet myself dared in poetry—changed me. Passing the words through one's own body, breath, and tongue *changes* one's relationship to language.

When I began work on *Danser sur tes braises* (published in 2020), I felt very far away from it. The previous book began with poetry and concluded with three lyric prose pieces. *Danser* begins with a visceral and painful series of prose journal entries, poem-like in their use of language. She was telling the story of the loss of her mother. Once more, I was on the other side of the divide, this time a divide of grief. I paused work on the book. Though I translated the poems that told of the pains of a thirty-year marriage, of the difficulties of parenthood, and of the experiences of menopause, the griefs of *Danser sur tes braises* were inaccessible to me.

Still, Devi and I communicated. I began publishing the translations. We collaborated on a project where she translated five of my poems, and we began a conversation about the act of translation. Then the unimaginable—unimaginable by me or by anyone—happened. My mother passed away. The details are not important. Or maybe they're everything. Regardless, I can't tell them yet. But I did go back to the texts of *Danser sur tes braises.* I could see them now. I could read them.

Devi's work is a shining beacon. One often heard about her that she was one of the most important voices in Indian Ocean literature, but truly, she is one of the most important voices in French literature and one of the most important voices in world literature, bar any border. It is hard in English—harder than you could imagine—to find her rhythms and sounds, and often what I do is approximate or relies on what English itself can offer. Considering that punctuation and a poetic line may also work *differently* in different languages, I've never been shy about "translating" those too. Devi, who speaks, reads, and writes perfect and fluent English, appreciates this way a translator must—always—take the text of the original into their own body and find the work anew. K.A.

Écrire est un acte monstrueux. Aucune décence par rapport aux secrets.

Toi mon eau trouble que je poursuis infiniment, indéfiniment pour mieux me soustraire à la clarté des souvenirs qui délayent et diluent la vérité, je le vois à présent, vous êtes trois:

l'inconnue qui a disparu de mon passé et du tien pour se dessiner, hasardeuse et perdue, dans l'oubli, et qui me regarde de ses yeux de lune meurtrie, à jamais en attente d'une quelconque vengeance – ta mère

toi, à qui je tente depuis tant d'années de dire adieu en m'équilibrant sur ton sourire et ta tristesse

et elle qui me double et me surplombe, qui m'élude et me définit, me donne ce visage parfois maléfique qui peuple ma nuit, m'éclaire au bouche-à-bouche des mots – moi.

Vous vous tendez la main parce que vous avez ceci de pareil: vous êtes fortes. Vous fendez votre chemin en ne cédant rien de vous-mêmes. Mon altière ego qui me regarde comme une sœur alors que j'escalade le versant de sa solitude. Mes alter égaux passant d'ombre en ombre sans aspirer à la lumière parce qu'elles n'ont que faire du bonheur.

Vous avez toutes compris que, parfois, les femmes remplissent tous leurs devoirs, sauf ceux qu'elles se doivent à elles-mêmes.

Ma femme agenouillée l'a compris: ne t'agenouille que parce que tu veux boire à la source du plaisir.

To write is a monstrous act. It has no respect for secrets. You, my troubled water I pursue relentlessly, endlessly, to better escape the clarity of memories that dilute and disperse the truth, I see it now: you are three:

the unknown who vanished from my past and from yours in order to draw herself dangerous and lost into oblivion, and who looks at me with her moon-marked eyes, forever in anticipation of some kind of vengeance—your mother

you, to whom I have been trying to bid farewell for so many years, suspended between your smile and your sadness

and the other, my twin, the one who hangs in front of me, who masks me and defines me, manifests this sometimes wicked face, haunts my night, who enlightens me, mouthing my words—me.

You reach out your hand to one another because you know you are strong. You hack your path through, ceding nothing. My lofty other who watches me like a sister while I climb the slope of her solitude. All my others creeping from the shade to more shade without ever aspiring to light because they want nothing to do with happiness.

You've understood everything: that sometimes women fulfill all their responsibilities except the ones they owe to themselves.

My kneeling woman knows: you kneel only in order to drink from the well of pleasure.

Devi . *From* Danser sur tes braises

Tu t'échappas du monde parce que tu avais renoncé à le conquérir. J'ai peur que tu ne sois partie, frappée d'incompréhension. Certaine que même tes filles étaient devenues des portes fermées. Il y avait entre nous ce vide qui provient du basculement des importances, de cette relativité qui ne concerne pas seulement le temps, mais également les émotions. Le regard que nous portions sur toi, et toi sur nous, était saisi de déphasage, d'astigmatisme. Nous ne savions plus ce que tu pensais de nous, nous étions toutes empêtrées dans ces remous de vie qui devenaient plus forts avec l'âge, nos vies d'adultes, nos soucis conjugaux ou parentaux, grand fleuve à sens unique qui te laissait loin derrière, même si tu voulais de toutes tes forces en être encore le tributaire.

Je crois que nous nous sommes enfoncées dans une sorte de folie purement féminine, avide et souterraine. Nous seules savons à quoi elle ressemble, lorsque nous la voyons au hasard du noir. Nous seules savons la nourrir de nos excès, de nos mourirs, parce que justement, nous portons, après la naissance de nos enfants, l'enfantement de notre mort. Alors se crée cette rivalité féminine, qui en sait plus sur l'autre, sur la manière dont la vie s'épuise et s'amenuise. Nous sommes obsidionales, carcérales. De plus en plus, nous sommes prises dans notre carcan de chair, dans nos murs introvertis, dans le ciment de nos doublures, et nous ne pouvons plus sortir. Nous sommes condamnées à la claustrophobie de notre être. Peut-être ne pouvons-nous que nous hanter les unes les autres par-delà la mort, par lignes interposées.

J'aurais voulu qu'il en soit autrement. Au fil de ces pages, je désespère de ma condition, voulue par moi.

You fled the world because you renounced the conquering of it. Though I am afraid, struck with confusion, you have not made your escape. Certain that even your daughters are closed doors now. There grew between us a gulf, the balance shifting, a relativity not only of time but of feelings. Our vision of each other blurred into near-sightedness. We didn't know anymore what you thought of us, we were caught in the eddies and swirls of life, growing stronger with age, our adult lives, our marital woes or parental difficulties, a great rushing current leaving you behind, bobbing in the distance even though you wanted with all your heart to once more be our tributary.

I think we've fallen into some kind of madness, purely feminine, greedy and subterranean. We only know what it looks like when we see it at random, black. We alone know to feed it with our excesses, with our deaths, because we know: after the birth of our children we bear the birth of our death. So this rivalry of women begins: who knows more about the other, who knows more about the way life exhausts itself and extinguishes. We are imprisoned, obsidian-like creatures. More and more, we are fastened in our shackles of flesh, in the walls closing in, lined in cement, with no way of escape. We are condemned to this claustrophobia. Maybe we can only haunt one another after death, in between the lines.

I wish it could have been otherwise. Throughout these pages, I despair my condition, though I wanted it.

Les arbres se fondent dans un enchevêtrement de bruns. C'est un matin gris, l'horizon est mouillé, brouillé, sans qu'il pleuve vraiment. À peine si les silhouettes se précisent dans l'éclair d'un feu; le soleil ne viendra pas.

Déjà l'automne. Dans l'avion qui attend de décoller pour Londres, je pense à cette autre partie du livre où je parle de Genève toute blanche sous la neige. Entre-temps sont passés un printemps et un été. Neuf mois, à peu près. Les couleurs précises des saisons: printemps lilas, été indigo. L'automne, lui, est une saison pleine d'emphase, jouant à la diva, prononçant d'une voix grave le décret de la mort des choses et des feuilles.

Ainsi, cela fera neuf mois que ce texte a été entamé, son écriture entrecoupée de longs intervalles où il m'était difficile d'y revenir. Neuf mois – c'est suffisant pour une genèse à l'échelle humaine. Plus que ça... Je ne sais pas. Tant de choses auraient pu se passer en ces quelques mois. Tant de choses se sont passées.

Mais qu'aurai-je appris?

The trees blur into a mess of brown. Gray morning, the horizon is drenched, watery, without actually raining. Shadows barely flaring into shape; the sun will not appear.

Autumn already. On the plane waiting to take off for London, I think of another part of the book where I wrote of Geneva completely white, covered by snow. In the meantime both a spring and a summer passed. Nine months, more or less. The precise colors of the seasons: lilac spring, indigo summer. Autumn is a season full of drama, playing at being a diva, pronouncing in a full voice the decree of the death of leaves and other things.

So, just like that it will be nine months since I began this text, its writing interspersed with long breaks where I couldn't bear to come back to it. Nine months—that's enough for a whole creation on human scale. More than that… I don't know. So many things could have happened in these few months. So many things did happen.

But what will I have learned?

Dès la naissance, la vie est une exploration de la perte.

Apprendre à perdre est la chose la plus difficile qui soit.

Ton visage, si grave. Ta main, même pas froide. Ton sari – le seul vêtement que tu portais – clair et frais. Ce ne sont pas là des images de mort. Ce sont celles d'une continuité, de liens préservés, de rêves encore et toujours arrimés à ta forme et à ton visage.

Bien sûr, le chemin n'est pas encore accompli. De ta mère à toi, de toi à moi, les entraves de la féminité ne se sont pas encore défaites, ni les énigmes résolues.

Peut-être appartient-il à une autre de nous libérer?

From birth, life is an exploration of loss.

The most difficult thing is learning to lose.

Your face—so serious. Your hand, not even cold. Your sari—the only clothing you wore—light and cool. These are not images of death. They are those of a line preserved, a line that continues, of dreams still and forever attached to your form and to your face.

Of course, the road has not yet ended. Of your mother to you, from you to me, the constraints of femininity are not yet undone, nor the mysteries yet solved.

Maybe it is someone else that will free us?

Tout commence par la perte des eaux. Et ce pacte, d'une chair à l'autre, devient un palimpseste, de femme en femme. De t'avoir parlé, à toi et à personne d'autre, j'ai l'impression d'avoir fait acte.

Cet acte innommé est une autre naissance. Mais est-ce la tienne ou la mienne? Ou celle de quelque descendante qui, loin dans le temps, regardera en arrière vers moi, son aïeule triste, et lui dira: tu n'as pas su vivre?

Qu'importe.

All time is unredeemable, a dit Eliot.

Impossible rédemption du temps.

It all begins with the loss of water. And this pact, of flesh to flesh, one to another, becomes a palimpsest, from woman to woman. Having spoken to you and no one else, I have the feeling of accomplishment.

This nameless act is another birth. But yours or mine? Or that of some descendant who, a long time from now, will look back at me, her sad ancestress, and say: didn't you know how to live?

No matter.

All time is irredeemable, I read in Eliot.

Impossible: to redeem time.

RAJ MOHAN

Songs from Sarnami

KANTRÁKI[1]

sát samundar pár karáy ke
ek nawá des ke sapná dekháy ke
kaise hamke u bharmáy ke
legail door Sarnám batáy ke

kaprá lattá kharchá gehná
gathri men bánh ke sab áshá
kirpá Sri Rám ke mutthi men
doosar ke sahárá páni pe
kabhi dil ghabráy, thorá pachhtáy
sáit ab jáy ke din barhyán áy
ánch suruj ke kuchh hamke bhi
bhág men mili, barsan tarsáy ke

dui teen mahinná jaháj pe
ristá nátá to ban hi jáy
kantrák jogáy ké thaili men
ek ek bichár dimágh men áy
u des men kaisan log bhentáy
kheti bári barhyán sairáy
pánch baris kaske kamáy ke
lautab gáon apan, paisá jamáy ke

kuchh din Sarnám men reh ke bhái
dhire dhire ádat par jáy
ab etná din mehnat kar ke
sab chhor chhár wápas ke jáy
jiw bole ab hinye reh jáy
sarkár ke bal pe khet mil jáy
man ke koná men i sapná baki
rahige ek din gáon apan jáy ke

---

[1]From: Bapauti/Erfenis (2006)
From the album *Kantráki*

CONTRACT LABOURER (INDENTURED LABOURER)

crossing over seven seas
promised a new land
how we were crimped by them
and taken to Surinam

clothing, food, jewelry
all hope bound in togs
with the blessing of God Rama in our hands
depending on strangers on the water
with some regret and pain in the heart
maybe better times will come now
after years of waiting
we too get some warmth of the sun

a few months together on the ship
mutual ties begin to grow
the contract safely packed away
all kinds of thoughts appear
what kind of people will we meet in that land
will the harvest be good
after five years of working hard and saving
I will return to my village

after such a long time in Surinam, brother
slowly one will get used to everything
now after having worked so hard
to leave everything behind and return
stay here says the heart
the state supports too with a piece of land
but in a corner of my heart
remains the dream of returning
to my village, one day

I TOR SAHAR

i tor sahar hai tor rastá
tor najar hai tor bát hai
tor jameen hai tor maṯṯi
tore nám ke jhandi khará hai
i tor dulár hai tor pardá
tor dharam hai tor bichár hai
i tor khusi hai tor marji
tor hisáb ke tor hissá hai

kab ayye hamár jameen ke maṯṯi
chhuwe tu
parchhaheen men baithe hamár
sune hál chál apan sunawe tu

bhágila apan peechhe
abbe torhe káran ham
baki kable kable kable kable
man ke bát sab sunilá
biná soche samjhe ham
baki kable kable kable kable
jáne kon káran tor háth
hamár hath men áyke chhutj̱á hai
jáne káhe rát hamár
rát se tor na mile hai

sáit tu sochat hoiye
ham sarek na báṯi
aýlá tor bahut nagichche
phusláwe tor man
mángat hoiye sáit abbe
ego kháli jagghá
ham duno ke bichche
kab ayye dhowáwe gor
rowandá ánkhi ke nichche
jáne kab ayye
kab ayye hamár jameen ke maṯṯi
chhuwe tu
parchhaheen men baithe hamár
sune hál chál apan sune tu

THIS IS YOUR CITY

this is your city, your path
your vision, your words
your turf, your earth
your flag, that sails so proudly, in your name
your love, your veil
your religion, your view
your (good) luck, your wants
your whole, your part.
when will you place your feet
on the floor from my ground,
sit in my shadow,
listen to my ups and downs,
share yours

I run after you
leaving myself behind
but for how much longer, how long, how long, how long
I follow my instincts.
don't even stop to think,
although I don't understand why
but for how much longer, how long, how long, how long
know not why your hand invariably
loses touch with mine
know not why
our nights never meet.
perhaps you think that I'm a fool,
coming too close to you,
to soothe your mind
maybe you still want
to keep a distance between us.
when will you bathe your feet
in the teardrops from my eyes?
tell me: when will you?

BIKÁW[2]

ladal bá tor denhi
jabran roke báte
apan penr ke pakkal phal
ras se bharal
agore hai turái khátin

ab heenche tu
khoj khoj ainá men
moori ke pakkal bár

bajár men tonhu lagáwal báte
khoob chikkan chamkáy ke
aur jhánk jhánk
toi toi ke toke
chhor dewe ek kaiti
aaj phino bachchi
bikri tor na bhail

ghari kab rukal ke ruki
roj dewe jantá gawáhi
ke umir tor ghate hai

abahyon hoi ját biyá
ta der ná rahat
abbe tu mái ban sake hai

[2]From: Bapauti/Erfenis (2006)

FOR SALE

your body is ready to burst
hold on tight with all your might
the ripe fruit from your tree
succulent, juicy
waiting to be plucked

already probing in the mirror
you pull out of your head
the odd grey hair

you too are on display in the marketplace
seriously dolled up
people look and
check you out from a distance
pass you by
again today girl
you've sealed no deals

as always the clock ticks onward
the public confirming everyday afresh
that you're becoming older and older

should you get married now
then it won't be too late
you can still become a mother

MÁNGILÁ[3]

mangila jiye jingi baki kaise
kaise chalab ham dui dui náv pe ek sanghe
daurab kab le sab ke peechhe apan bichaar se hatke

ján boojh ke ultá rastá chalilá
chhor chhár rit-o-riváj bhágilá
door koi khet jahán pandit na bole hai
mái na rowe palwár na roj roj
táná sunáve hai
dhim táná dere táná dere táná dhim
tánánána táná dere táná

kable i jingi jar djarigá i des ke matti men
kasie bachábe boli bhásá sau jáát ke bichche men
chál dhál dusre ke ápan mánilá
dál bhát chokhá se nátá toorilá
lád phán ke purkhan ke sab riváj
doono kandhá pe áj
daphnáyla rowat samundar ke páni men
dhim táná dere táná dere táná dhim
tánánána táná dere tán

[3]From: Tihá/Troost (2010)
(Composed by Raj Mohan for the CD Daayra)

MÁNGILÁ

I want to lead my own life
but how
how can I sail opposing ships simultaneously
how can I travel diverging
paths together
how long must I chase after others
keeping my own beliefs at a distance

deliberately, I tread
the opposite path
walking away from rituals and traditions
towards a remote land
where the priest doesn't preach
mothers never grieve
family refrains from criticizing

how much longer must I wait
before my life takes root
in this land
how will I save my own culture
locked in between a hundred other races
values and ethics of another
I make my own
breaking my bonds
with rice, lentils, and pate
traditions from my ancestors
I bind up around both shoulders
and, tearfully, bury them at sea

TORE DULÁR[4]

tore dulár ke ánch se
chulhá bare hai
tore ánchal ke hawá se
ánkhi lage hai
tore ánkhi ke jyoti se
anjor rahe hai
tore kangan ke áwáj se
saber jage hai

sooch bichár ke gauná hoige
jur gail nátá tor sáth
denhi ke sab soná galge
tor denhi ke ánch men
chup cháp baithal báte
jhalwá ke bagle
kab jhoolab ham sanghe
kab jhoolab hawá men sáthe

tore háth ke rekhá se
takdeer hamár bahe

---

[4]From the album *Kantráki* and book *Bapauti/Erfenis*

YOUR LOVE

by your love's warmth
the clay oven burns
by the breeze of your waving scarf
I fall asleep
by the light in your eyes it remains light
by the tinkling of your bracelets
the morning awakens

my thoughts yet young are married off
I am connected with you
all the gold in my body has melted
by your body's warmth
you are sitting a bit quiet
besides the swing
when are we going to swing together
when are we going to swing together in the wind
through the lines in your hand
flows my fate

Photograph by Andil Gosine

KEVIN JARED HOSEIN

It Takes Courage

Peter Badree was a stocky man, only forty years old, his head grey as a chinchilla. He wore a unibrow, almost proudly, and had curls of hair springing from his knuckles. You could tell he was once a handsome young man. Since he was twenty-three, he had worked as a taxi driver. Two months ago, he won a case against the Office of the Attorney General. The police had detained his vehicle for reckless driving. Peter was never given a court date or any means to contest the citation. For thirty-eight months, his livelihood was locked away, deteriorating in the Sea Lots impound. The defense lunged with fangs that aimed to sink deep into Peter's character, saying that he seldom ran his taxi's designated legal route (while he still had it) and that even when he did work, he wasn't a consistent worker. Oh yes, ladies and gentlemen of the jury, Peter Badree is a lazy, incompetent deadbeat who has never paid taxes. They inveigled his brother-in-law into testifying against his moral fibre to lay before the jury that he regularly drank, brawled, and gambled now. That he religiously neglected his three children. That his house along its lonely stretch on Todds Road was in disarray. And that an alcoholic of his temperament should not be allowed to work in the public transport service.

It was true. Peter had hit the bottle hard. He'd turned to gambling and horse races, and his children's school supply money was now in some slot machine in the lobby of a Chinese restaurant. Everything he and his wife had put together in fifteen years was dismantled in a matter of weeks. Peter's family, which was manageable before the incident, became destitute. Peter's own rebuttal to all of this was that the police and every authority he encountered during these thirty-eight months defeated his spirit, and he had lost all will to work. It takes more than ambition to keep on the straight and narrow after you've been blindsided and knocked off course, the prosecutor told the jury. We have all encountered misfortune and unfairness. We all know how difficult life is—not just life, but livelihood. How about we make it easier for one man? In every case I've ever come across, you have two parties. The wrong and the wronged. It is now your job to decide which is which.

For this, Peter received close to half a million dollars in punitive and special damages. The first thing he did was sign up for a credit card. The first purchase he made was a necklace, each cultured pearl harvested from akoya oysters halfway around the world. The second purchase was a Magic Bullet blender for his wife.

***

Jaikrishnan Dayabhai (J. D.) Lalit worked at the counter of Bakery & Bits. The establishment and brand were owned by his uncle. J. D. mainly had the job because his uncle wanted him to stay out of trouble. He was polite, helpful, and (most would say) very good at his job. That fella could convince a diabetic to buy a dozen jam tarts, his uncle said. He talked to almost everyone who came into the store, balancing between being intrusive and being amusing. He also knew when not to speak. He'd gotten in trouble a few times for giving away cupcakes to girls he liked. His uncle warned him and made him pay for each one. When he stopped giving away the cupcakes, the girls stopped giving him attention.

During this time, he became acquainted with an eight-year-old boy named Hemant Badree. Hemant was Peter Badree's middle child. Every Tuesday and Friday, the boy would ride up in his bicycle with money for about a dozen loaves—white, wholewheat, lemon, and cinnamon. As the boy packed the loaves into a backpack, J. D. asked the boy what he was going to do with all that bread. The boy explained that he took orders for deliveries, for which he was paid a dollar each. He said he was fed up with being poor and had come up with a way to do something he enjoyed (riding his bicycle) while making a few extra dollars for the week. His remarks were without wit, and J. D. was astounded by the boy's straightforward admission. He admired the boy's honesty so much that he threw in a custard pastry into the batch each time after that. It became routine. J. D. teased him about girls at school, chatted about football, and traded gossip about teachers. For a brief moment in the evenings, he felt like a big brother. This went on for about a year.

After Peter Badree won his case, Hemant stopped taking deliveries and, thus, stopped coming to the bakery. J. D. felt petty to admit it—he felt slighted. The boy barely acknowledged him now. On his way home, J. D. spotted the boy showing off his new Google Pixel 4 to his friends. Who were these friends? J. D. wondered. He had never seen them before. Hemant had never spoken of them. The boy had mainly spoken—and spoken candidly—of boys making fun of him for not having money. Hemant had always been the smelly poor boy from the smelly Badree clan. The boy with only one stained school shirt with the frayed collar. The boy didn't even have a rag to wipe his nose. Were these boys the same boys? Now they were recording videos of themselves trying to do bottle flips and dabbing. J. D. felt more than slighted when he saw this. He was jealous. He saw a part of himself in Hemant's struggle. Now Hemant could put it behind him. J. D. couldn't and most likely never would be able to.

J. D. had been working at his uncle's bakery for two years and could never afford a phone like that. The more he thought about it, the more he resented the job—and his position in life. He'd never had aspirations to become someone great, but it bothered him that nobody cared to be friends with him when he wasn't behind the counter. He had wasted so much time believing that people respected him. All these worthless people. They only ever liked him when he was behind the counter, looming behind a glass case of confections that now made him want to vomit.

Courier trucks hurled up and down the dusty road, Amazon boxes bumping into each other, packed with makeup, trinkets, video games, and whatever else the Badree family could now afford. Gayatri, the daughter, now wore twill utility pants and flounce tops from Forever 21. The youngest, Niti, had a new pair of AirPods and Big Kid huarache sneakers. Outside the Badree house were towers of discarded cardboard boxes plastered with Samsung, Sony, Hewlett-Packard, Bose, Lenovo.

One day, J. D. followed Hemant as he went to meet his friends. He was hugging a bucket of Kentucky Fried Chicken against his chest the way a schoolgirl would carry her textbooks. One of his friends asked him, Where do get the money to buy that?

Suitcase, Hemant said.

Suitcase? another asked.

Yes, Hemant replied. I go under the bed sometimes and take what I need. Pa don't have to know.

***

Mangal and Mukesh didn't live in the area. They were twins and were inseparable. And that's how they were always referred to by their teachers, their neighbours, parlour clerks—Mangal-and-Mukesh, never the other way around. They were tall, had an equal amount of brawn, and shaved their beards with hot kitchen knives. They lived in an abandoned shipping container at the side of the highway with their mother. Mangal, when he was little, liked to play-bite his mother. Mukesh later adopted the habit, as if he drew the power from his brother. Their mother was never fond of them and blamed them for everything. If a bulb blew, they got the belt. If rats got to the bread or a stray dog shat at their doorstep, they got the belt. When Mangal picked up smoking, so did Mukesh. When Mukesh dropped out of school, so did Mangal. J. D. was their classmate from primary school. They had bullied J. D. for his money. J. D. became fed up one day and hurled an insult at one of them, calling him an ugly buzzard. He couldn't remember which one he directed the words at or if it mattered. An assault on one was an affront to the other.

Mangal-and-Mukesh dragged skinny J. D. out to a scrubby glade surrounded by crabwood and quinam guava, made him strip down to his bare bottom and walk a mile and a half down the station road in the rippling heat back to his house. J. D. sometimes reflected on that day, still astonished by the eldritch power they held over him. They had neither lifted a finger at him nor threatened violence if he disobeyed—yet his clothes were in a pile on the ruffled dirt as if they were foliage naturally shed from a tree. J. D. stayed out of the twins' way but became fixated on them after that incident. He supposed that everyone who crossed their path felt the same to some degree.

The brothers sometimes spoke in unison, taking turns as each other's echo. They had their meals together. They drank and smoked the same brands. They lurked together outside of the guesthouse behind the riverside pub, so they could catch a glimpse of the girls when they came out of their rooms to smoke. They each had had only one sexual encounter—it was with the same girl, Renuka Mahabir. J. D. knew Renuka. She told him it was only a curious physical tryst. They are two angry boys, she told him. Eighteen and bored and filled with wrath for all people. When she turned them down the following time, they took no disrespect. They were picked up by the police a few times for fighting. Remember Sarran from school? she asked. I think them is the reason he can't breathe good now. They didn't attend their mother's funeral and cremation when she died, didn't cry, and didn't shave their heads. J. D. was one of the few to visit them during this time. He brought a six-pack of Stag with him.

Let's go start somethin, J. D. said. The brothers always occupied the backseat, sitting hip-to-hip. They drove up to Maracas Valley, parked near a bridge, and blasted Machine Head and Fear Factory. They headbanged under the screech of cicadas until well after midnight. J. D. became good friends with Mangal-and-Mukesh after that, and whenever he said those words, Let's go start something, they did. When they ran out of money, they beat up and robbed drunks and sissy boys and pooled together the spoils for more beer.

One night, when they were all drunk, J. D. suggested that they break into Peter Badree's house and steal his suitcase of money. He had his livelihood taken away for thirty-eight months. We ain't never had no livelihood! J. D. exclaimed into the dark bushes. Mangal-and-Mukesh nodded in unison. Money would be nice. The three began to scheme. It was the first time any of them would do something like this. They mugged, drag-raced on the highway, and hot-wired cars for fun, but they knew that none of this was on the level of a home invasion. This is the kind of thing you would either celebrate or regret forever, J. D.'s inebriated mind knew.

On the weekends, at five p.m., Peter would leave the house, not returning until eleven. The paint was flaking off the doors of his car, and it had significantly depreciated since its detention. Still, the car ran well after a tune-up, and Peter had no plans to purchase a new one. Why sell your luckiest possession? They followed him three times—Friday, Saturday, and Sunday—and the three times his destination was the same. Regal Heart Villas. J. D. knew of the place. So did Mangal-and-Mukesh, but they never admitted it to him. J. D. always had his hair cut at the barbershop next door, where the barbers openly spoke to each other about how a man hasn't lived until he's tasted pink peaches at least once in his life. They'd have open debates on which one was the best—was it Sofia from San Cristobal, Elena from Barranquilla, or Kristina from right here in Freeport? J. D. always suspected that the two businesses were affiliated.

Peter Badree never stayed for long at the orange-painted stucco brothel—perhaps ten minutes for the most. Whenever he left, his passenger seat was occupied. Only once did they follow him. He drove all the way up to Port-of-Spain. A fair young woman stepped out of the car—her chequered skirt and red ribbons in her hair making her look like a schoolgirl. In sharp contrast was the pearl necklace that looked like it instead belonged around the neck of an old, stately socialite. Peter took her to an Italian restaurant along the savannah that looped the soundtrack of a tarantella. They drank chianti and ate antipasti on little plates. They walked out with a bottle of brunello, popped it on the sidewalk, and began taking swigs of it right there. Their drive continued to a long stretch of road in Chaguaramas, where the derelict British West Indies aircraft from the military museum was still visible. They parked on the side of the road and wandered down to the banks, taking the brunello with them. She laid her head on his lap while he stroked her hair, both of their shadows blending into the thick sea. They stole kisses from each other. These aren't the kind of kisses you pay for, J. D. thought. They kissed like in the movies. The boys watched them for half an hour, leaving before the two could finish their bottle.

On the way back, J. D. decided that the following Saturday at ten p.m. would be best. Mangal-and-Mukesh nodded in agreement. J. D. cautiously explained the terms of the plan. He would act as a lookout and getaway driver. He stressed that he would not be physically involved with the scene inside the house, given that he would be easily recognized. The twins would wear masks and, under no circumstance, should use names. Absolutely no guns. They would do this with cutlasses, rope, and duct tape. And there must be no bodies. At the first sign of trouble, they must abandon the plan.

***

Saturday night was slow to come. On more occasions than he cared to remember, customers from the bakery asked J. D. if he was feeling alright—that he looked ill. He didn't bother to feign politeness. He had already left these people behind. In his mind, the suitcase of money was already his. He just had to go pick it up. Earlier that day, J. D. let Mangal-and-Mukesh practice binding him with the rope, though they both forgot as quickly as they learned. When five p.m. finally came, he drove along Todds Road to make sure that Peter was gone. When he went to get Mangal-and-Mukesh from their shipping container home, they weren't ready. Usually, they would be out sitting on the grass. Only when J. D. double-tapped the horn did they emerge. They already had their ski masks on.

Take those damn things off, J. D. said. Only when you out the car, you put them on.

They were on Todds Road by minutes to ten. Peter Badree was still out. Only when J. D. cut the headlights did it become apparent how dark the night was. Darkness on all sides of the hill. A skyline of black, weeping trees. The silhouette of the rolling hills is almost mathematical in nature. The sparsely lit house became the only real thing in the whole world at that moment. The only sound was the slow burn of insects. There were no houses either way for at least a minute's drive. J. D. looked at the brothers through the rearview.

Remember. Three children, one woman, he said to the brothers. You have to move fast. Make sure they don't call nobody. Make sure they don't run away. I gonna be right here in case anyone manage to get out of the house. If you have to slap someone to get them to behave, go ahead. If you have to chop the woman, go ahead—but make sure you hit an arm or a leg. No head, no chest. We not taking lives. Just that suitcase. If you hear me honk, get the hell out and we'll drive the hell outta here.

Mangal-and-Mukesh put on their masks and slipped their cutlasses down the rear of their jeans. They did it like it was business as usual, business all the time. Mangal opened the door, but Mukesh put his hand on his brother's shoulder. Mangal stopped, and they closed their eyes for a few seconds, as if offering a prayer, before continuing on their way. They scaled the chain-link fence and, in just two seconds, were in the yard. Keeping low, they made their way to an open window and climbed in. As they vanished from J. D.'s sight, it appeared as if the house had swallowed them. An igneous panic set into J. D.'s gut, a thick, congested bolus that hardened like cooled black magma.

The house remained as it was—J. D. half-expected the two-story structure to collapse once the family occupying it realized what was happening to them.

A car appeared in the distance. Its headlights are like two stars fallen from the sky and wafting down the hill. J. D. took a breath as the lights rose and swelled, blooming before his face. He raised his sleeve over his eyes as the car approached, the dread in him settling in long, shuddering waves. The car slowed as it rode past his window. J. D. kept his sleeve up and forcefully hunched against his seat.

Two minutes later, the front light went out—what J. D. reckoned was the living room.

What was happening in there? J. D. half-wished for some kind of crystal ball or portal he could gaze into. He imagined himself in the situation as a child. He projected his actions onto the Badree children. Hide under the bed and hold your breath. Press your body into the hardwood floor until you sank into the house. Don't think about life or death. In situations like this, you don't make a sound, even if the shadows were to get you—that way, you wouldn't know if you're dead or alive. Let yourself go numb like the minutes before surgery. Maybe you'll awaken. Maybe you'll remain asleep.

A screaming cracked through the darkness, and the side light went out as well. The house was now outlined with the pale glow of a ghost. J. D. had regrets now. He turned to his hand, fingers splayed out like roots, hovering two inches from the car horn as if to ward off a blow. It was stuck that way, and he had to lean his entire body forward to hit the horn. Out blared a bizarre klaxon, first loud and then cracking like the compressed pitch of an eunuch, a sign that J. D. understood meant the battery could give out at any moment. He leaned into the passenger seat, waiting to see the shadows of Mangal-and-Mukesh emerge from the front door. He wasn't even thinking about the suitcase anymore.

But there was nothing. Instead, another scream burst out. J. D. slammed his hand down on the horn again. This one weakly zipped over the grassy hill, where it was castrated by the dark.

J. D. got out of the car and climbed the fence. He cut his palm on the way down. It was so dark that he couldn't see how bad the cut was—it looked like a messy black line running from thumb to wrist. He went around the side of the house, where there was still light. The lone lit window looked like a big, bright square suspended in mid-air. The drapes were pulled, but through the slit, he could see Hemant's little brother, Niti, and his big sister, Gayatri, sitting against their bedroom wall, hands bound behind their backs, their mouths duct-taped shut. Niti was furiously shaking his head. His sister was breathing so fast that her torso went springy. She had a gash above her eye, and blood was beginning to pool into her lower eyelid.

A loud clanging sound came from the other side of the house, and light came back to the living room. J. D. darted over to the living room window, crouching so low that the bridge of his nose touched the sill. Hemant was on the floor, face-down, his head surrounded by a mess of pot shards. The burnished brown carpet became darker and darker as the seconds passed. Time slowed down here, and J. D.'s mind was ripped in half.

He could help this family. Or he could flee.

Celebration. Or regret.

Mrs. Badree let out an anguished yell, running to her son, nearly tripping on a footstool. Her nightie had been ripped right down to her mid-back. J. D.

angled his eyes to the corner of the room, where Mangal-and-Mukesh stood, shoulders sloping and languid like two scolded infants.

Mrs. Badree's face was big and wrinkled now. It reminded J. D. of a pumpkin. She ran into the bedroom and came back with a gun—a black and silver Smith and Wesson. Mangal saw her, but Mukesh didn't—his eyes were on the boy on the floor, who was beginning to convulse. Mrs. Badree had to shoot three times before getting Mukesh in the head. His body fell on the boy's. Mangal ran up to Mrs. Badree with his cutlass drawn and brought it down upon her arm. She fired as her fingers disconnected from her body. Piece of the ceiling fell. The gun and her fingers were at the foot of a shelf.

Mangal drew a knife out of his sock and stabbed Mrs. Badree in her collar. She rolled over, screaming out. She held her palm out—an unnatural, raw disc of flesh without its phalanges. He kept stabbing, his motions almost gentle, tender, bringing the knife down on her flanks and back like they were a lover's massage. He was sobbing while he did it. J. D. had never heard someone scream like Mrs. Badree did for the final minute of her life. It was so horrid that J. D. imagined it as some other sound—a kettle going off, a schoolbell, a firework. Like when you repeat a word so often, it paradoxically loses familiarity. When the screams turned to sputters, J. D. could make out Mangal's saying: that's it there boy that's it there boy that's it there boy...

In the other room, the two children were howling. Mama! Mamaaa! Ohhhh mamaaa! Those weren't children; J. D. tried to convince himself. Those were goats tied to bedposts. He clutched the apron of the window, immobile, as if he were stuck in a diving bell plummeting towards the ocean floor. Mangal didn't stop. He kept stabbing the body long after it went silent. His entire chest was drenched with red when he went to check on his brother, a single hole above his eyebrow. No exit wound.

Mangal picked up the gun, put it in his mouth, and pulled the trigger.

J. D. fell to the ground. At first, he thought he had finally regained the strength to move—until he felt the boots on his neck. His chin pressed down hard against the gravelly dirt, and he spotted the headlights from Peter Badree's car behind the open gate. Dust fell into the light like snow.

Peter Badree took J. D. into the house by his ears. Midway to the house, J. D.'s car keys fell out of his pocket. With a quick swipe, the man picked up the keys and flung them over the fence and into some bushes. His face was like a black hole until they came into the house. His children were still screaming from the back room. Mr. Badree froze in shock at the sight of his wife's body. It looked as if she'd been dipped into a well of blood.

J. D. took this moment of respite to break free.

He kicked the man in his shin and bolted out of the house. He made it to the road, and only the darkness of night was before him. The insects in humming speculation. The utility poles static as toys. He couldn't remember the moment when he heard the children's screaming stop. Suddenly, there was light behind him. The rattle and rumble of rubber and metal. With nothing to see before him, it felt like he was getting nowhere. No sense of direction, no sense of position. He prayed, oh God, please, oh God, please, to meet another set of lights coming from the opposite direction. Two fallen stars. I am sorry, God. Please save me, oh God. Just send another soul, some buffer between me and the reaper. But no one came. It was like he was in another world, one constructed just for judgment.

He turned, making a dash for the bushes, but Mr. Badree already had him. He couldn't fight him off. As soon as he batted one hand away, it was like two more latched onto him. His shadow wasn't human anymore. Who could be human after what went down tonight? Mr. Badree shoved him into the car and drove him back up the hill to the house. It was fully illuminated now.

He pushed J. D. past the bodies and the purling pools of blood in the living room. He pushed him from one nightmare into the next. In the children's bedroom, the children's hips were still touching, but their bodies were slumped on opposite sides in the shape of a discarded maple seed. A massacred butterfly. The girl was already at rest, her temple blown out raw. The little boy was slumped to the side, still breathing, trying hard to hold onto life, the red blotch on his shirt quickly eating his chest. The only thing that seemed to keep the boy alive for his final minutes was his sheer confusion, trying to find the right words or thoughts for what happened. J. D., as well. But he didn't wonder for long—the bullet ripped through his mouth, and he vomited smoke. His eyes remained locked with the boy's, the light going out in them both as Mr. Badree stabbed himself in the leg and rehearsed his story in the next room.

JAY AJA

Generational Trauma Is A Weapon

When most people think of comics, they imagine superheroes and villains, a staple of mainstream media. Yet the more nuanced truth is that comics as a genre is an expansive storytelling medium capable of embodying all types of narratives and histories. For example, poetry comics as a subgenre has existed for a while and is becoming more recognizable alongside graphic novels, graphic memoirs, literary comics, and modern comic strips. I chose to create "Generational Trauma Is A Weapon" in the form of a poetry comic as a method of combining my visual art process with my poetry practice. Incorporating images of items and memories I grew up with alongside artifacts in the form of old family photographs, I sought to introduce a textural element in recreating my history growing up as a second-generation-immigrant Guyanese, experiencing the legacy of my family as one descended from Caribbean indentureship.

windy day spent
holding the small
continents of sweetsop

I'm often surprised
by the things Dad grows
in the driveway of a FL HOA

suburbia, so far away
from Guyana, where he learned
to plant the soil, to feed
hungry, skinny bodies, collecting
water for unfillable holes, demanding
more, more, always **more**

I wondered if that's how he saw us...

before the HOA, was the split-
level house Dad bought in the '80s
real estate bubble, threatening to pop
by the time I was born
in the '90s. There were fruit
trees, citrus, plums, bananas,
and there was us:
Didi, Brother, and me,
we were a bounty, too

in the backyard was Dad's Guyana
cherry bush Mom said would never bear
but every season after was a riot

of red berries like small pumpkins
I shoved into my jack-ó-lantern mouth,
hiding behind the sugar cane, thick like whips

as Dad begins to cuss out Mom, remember
Mamoo's fear in picking his switch, Nana
plying his cutlass to cut the rod

it's supposed to be a funny story
Mamoo's eyes as he thinks of the blows,
laughing, the way only trauma can make you

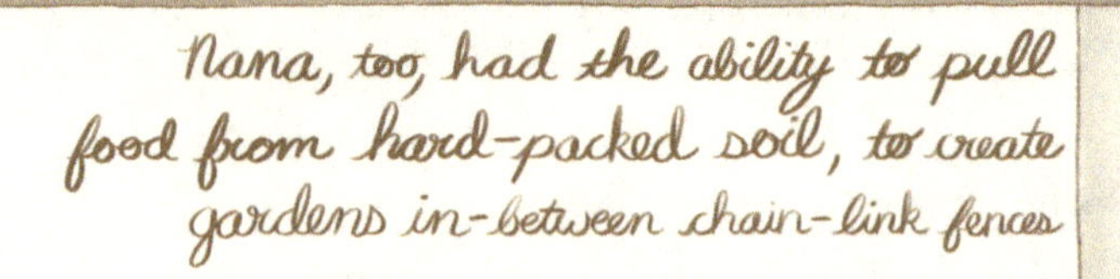

in Little Guyana, imagine my surprise
to discover his hands, once balled fists
proffered up to Mom's face,

Generational trauma
is the weapon
passed down
from open mouth
to open mouth,
unfilled and yearning,
often too much
to feed, so it takes,
and yes, people
are a garden to uproot,
even children,
yes, spaces
where seeds
are never planted

in the kitchen was a bottle of Black Label
Dad drank from every night, the sweet amber
whiskey a lighthouse calling him home
through the dark, I felt its pull, it took me
a while to understand the ways Dad self-soothed

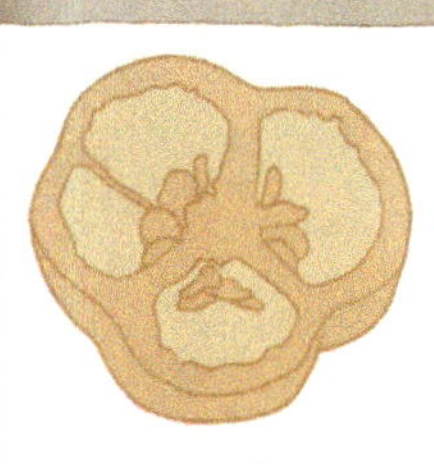

in the front yard grew scotch

bonnet, habaneros, wiri wiri peppers

Dad ate like candy, inviting neighbors

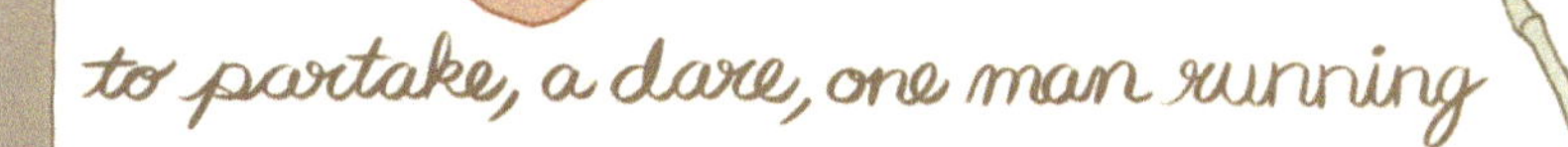

to partake, a dare, one man running

all the way home to slake the heat

with orange juice, got pepper in his eyes,

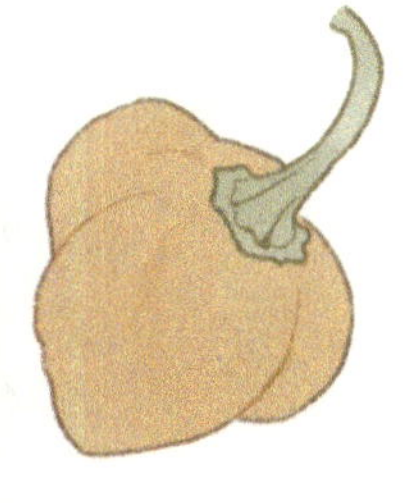

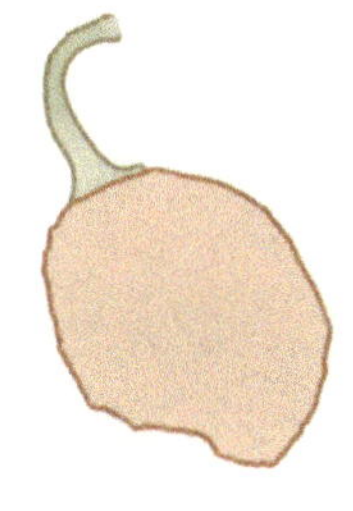

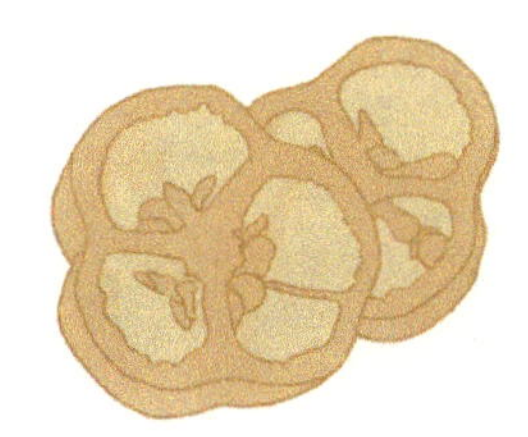

it's burning and Dad's laughing, his tongue,

his throat, the deadened skin

cells, all lost feeling a long time ago

Indentureship is a legacy
I don't entirely understand,

have had the privilege to forget,

my American birth certificate in hand,
yet I still see the effects, in Nana

the family stories of the beatings

he inflicted on Nani in Guyana,
the hard days, the long sun, Dad

reaching for the grip of the cutlass

when I wake him to ask a question
and he lets it drop, realizing there is no threat

I want to tell him the story of Nana
and the thief, in the moonless night

how Nana snatched up his cutlass

and gave chase, the thief running unseen,
a shadow in the dark, mirroring Nana,

and show him my hand,

explain it is a kind of land
from which an Amazon sprouted

with water in-between, spread

the fingers to show there is
no jumbie in the night

just fear, with a way of crossing
borders

in the fridge is a paper bowl Dad filled
for me with sweetsop, calling me to eat

and I do, pulling at the soft skin, so ripe
it slides open, unveiling the eye of a seed,

dark and shiny, encased in a cataract of white
and I understand the circumference

of a lifetime built on shaky foundations
is theirs with no bridge across

the years, only seeds, to put forth

Photograph by Andil Gosine

Devotional Songs from Surinam and Trinidad

TRANSLATED BY RAJIV MOHABIR

These songs fall under the category of Tān-Singing or Baithak Gāna and represent what ethnomusicologists call "local classical music" from the East Indian communities of the Caribbean. The recordings of these songs were made available through YouTube and are all from the 1970s, as that was the heyday of Tān-Singing as a genre. This local genre of music is stylized and represents a diasporic creation—innovative iterations of music that are semiclassical in that they are not Hindustani or Carnatic, nor folksong, but a new genre altogether, Indo-Caribbean. I read them as important postcolonial Caribbean texts: poems put to music in keeping with the South Asian tradition of poems incarnating as songs. Because of this, I think it necessary to show my translation journey, first into Guyanese Creole, two generations removed from me—the Creole I use is that of my grandparents' generation in Berbice.

The authorship of these songs remains dubious in that each iteration through performance sees changes in the lyrics. They are superficially attributed to the medieval poet-saint Kabir, while the songs from "Muslim Inspiration" are by and from Jameer Hosein and Harry Mahabir. Following this tradition, I am ascribing authorship to each performer.

The text of the songs for "O Priyatam" is from a recording of the Surinamese Ramdew Chaitoe in 1976 on the album "The Star Melodies of Ramdew Chaitoe." A version of this song was translated by Chutneymusic.com but this translation is my own.

Trinidadian Sharm Yankaran's father, Rakesh Yankaran, came to the Caribbean from Andhra Pradesh. "The Washerman" represents devotional texts in music and makes reference to Kabir. In a local Caribbean convention authorship is often ascribed in such texts to the poet Kabir (1400s and 1500s ACE). This was recorded in 1979 in Trinidad.

The songs "Please God" and "This Is My Message" both come from the Jameer Hosein and Harry Mahabir recording called "Muslim Inspiration" from Trinidad by Windsor Records in 1973.

O PRIYATAM

As performed by Ramdew Chaitoe

हो प्रियतं प्यारे तू कहाँ बसत है
मोहे नगरिया बता जा

तोहरे संदेसा मैं कउन से पूछूँ
कउन नगरिया मैं जाउ
मोहे डगरिया बता जा

बनके कोयलिया जंगलवा में ढूँढूँ
बनके मछरिया जमुनवा में ढूँढूँ
मोहे जंगलवा बता जा
मोहे जमुनवा बता हा

मोहे नगरिया बता जा

काबे में ढूँढ़ा मदीने में ढूँढ़ा
कासी में ढूँढ़ा मधुबन मैं ढूँढ़ा
कोई मन्दिरवा बता जा
कोई मस्जिदवा बता जा

मोहे नगरिया बता जा
हो प्रियां तू कहाँ बसत है
मोहे डगरिया बता जा

O PRIYATAM

O Saiya, whe' you gan an' live
whe' you deh
Wha' town you deh in

Who me can ask, who go tell meh
de road you walk
til wha' side you gan

You mus' 'e turn into de twa twa
into de burd wha' de in de farest

You mus' 'e turn into de fish
wha' swim in de Jamuna

Wha' jungle and bush you gan in
wha' rivah and trench you de in

Me come from de Kabbah side
me been go a Medina come

Me gan a Kasi
me come back from Madhubanwa

Wha' kine mandir mein you go deh inside
wha' masjid you deh in

O tell me where me mus' go
whe' you gan an' live
whe' you deh

O PRIYATAM

O Saiya, Priyatam
where do you dwell
Tell me the town

Who can I ask for news of you
which town should I visit
which road you took

Have you transformed
into a jungle cuckoo

Have you become
a fish in the Jamuna river

Tell me which jungle
Tell me where in the Jamuna

I went as far as the Kabbah
searched as far as Medina

I traveled all the way to Kashi
and came from as far as Madhuban

Tell me which temple
which masjid

Tell me where you are now
which town should I visit
which road I should take

THIS WASHERMAN

As performed by Sharm Yankaran

धोबिया जल ही में मरता पियासा

जल में थार पिये नहीं मूरख
अच्छा जल है खासा
अपना घर मरम ना जाने
करे धोबिया के आसा

जल बीच मरता पियासा

छिन में धोबिया रोवे धोवे
छिन में रहे उदासा
आपे बंधे करम की रस्सी
आपन गर के फ़सा

जल बीच मरता पियासा

सच्चा साबुन लेही ना मूरख है
संतान के पासा
दाग पुनारा छुतत नहीं
धोवत बारहमासा

जल बीच मरता पियासा

एक राती को जोरी लगावे
छोरी दिये भारी मासा
कहे कबीर सुनो भाई साधो
आचत अन्ना उपासा

जल बीच मरता पियासा

THIS WASHERMAN

Even doh 'e deh, stand in de wata
hiya to yahso
'e go tursty an' dead

De stupid man ke foot deh in de trench
an' de wata clean
but 'e na tek 'am ke drink
de dhobi jus' wash 'e kapra plenty

Watch 'e go cry an' cry
an' den 'e mout' go suske
'e go mek de rope fe heng 'e self

'E na go tek da same sense
de pandit does talk in ' katha
chunariya mein lagal daag
you cyan wash out dat daag

All de strengt' 'e get 'e use 'am
one time
an' punish bad de nex' time

Hear bhaiya, Kabir seh
you get flowa but na mek roti

THIS WASHERMAN

Standing in the water
        the washerman dies of thirst

Ankle deep the fool doesn't drink
        but the water is clean
He doesn't know water builds the house
        he just washes and washes

In an instant he cries without control
        the next his grief is loud
He himself braids the rope he places
        around his neck

The soap of truth he doesn't bring
        the soap all the saints have and use
The aged stain doesn't wash out though
he washes it over and over for twelve months

For a single night he uses all his strength
        and forgets the other work he must do
Says Kabir, listen brothers and saints
        though grains are full, you starve

PLEASE GOD

As performed by Jameer Hosein and Harry Mahabir

کرلو خدا کو رازی میرے بھای بہنوں
،ہے وہ خدا تمہارا دل جا سے وسکا پوجا

وہ ،ہے تمہارا کالمکی وس سے کرلو
وہ چاہتا ،ہے تمکو تم کیا سے وسے کرلو

بچوں سے اپنا بیٹھٹ کر ،ہے پل وہ تمکو
اسے پیار رب کو کیوں اپ بھولتے ہو

باسخت مکت سے جاوں بہتریہی ہے تجھکو
مرنے سے پہلے اپنے رازی تو کر خدا کو

PLEASE GOD

Mek God happy, me buddy an' sistren
Da na you god? So mus' puja wid you heart

Wha' you get na you one foreveah, so love good
He wan' you fe rememba dis na you one

You baite ke wid you pickni dem
But you faget fe sit wid Rab like dis

Be strong an' de strengt' 'e go gi- ayou go deh good
Before you gan, you mus' mek God happy

PLEASE GOD

Please God, O my brothers and sisters
He is your God, worship him with all your heart

What is yours is yours for a time; love wholly
He wants you; what do you really do with this time

You sit with your children; that moment is yours
Why do you forget to love God like this

Go with strength, it is better for you
Before you die, please and satisfy God

THIS IS MY MESSAGE

As performed by Jameer Hosein and Harry Mahabir

میرا پیغام تم سن لو اگر مرضی تمہاری ہو
خدا کو پوجو دل سے تم اگر مرضی تمہاری ہو

وہ گئی کالک تمہارا ہے وہ اللہ تمہارا ہے
بنالو اپنا نہ تم وسکو اگر مرضی تمہاری ہو

محمد آدم عیسیٰ موسیٰ رب کو پوجا تھے آئی
وسکو اپ اتی پوجو اگر مرضی تمہاری ہو

اگر مسلمان ہو ولفت کے رکھے چھڑو
کر ولفت خدا دے تم اگر مرضی تمہاری ہو

THIS IS MY MESSAGE

Hear me na, if you wan'.
    Mek du'a wid you heart if you wan'.

Wha' gan, gan, dis time you get you one;.
    mek Allah 'am yours if you wan'

Mohammad, Adam, Jesus, Moses, all come
    an' puja Allah. You mus' do 'am too if you wan'

If you Musalman mus' lef' all de worl'
    for de love you give Khuda, if you wan'.

THIS IS MY MESSAGE

Attend to my message if you desire.
With heart pray to Khuda, if you desire.

What was, is gone, now this time is yours,
Allah is yours, make him yours, if you desire.

Mohammed, Adam, Jesus, Moses, all came
to worship God. Worship him too if you desire.

Be you Muslim, abandon all for this love,
for this love of Khuda, if you desire.

7 Daggers

The second time   you open my legs you press
your middle finger to my blue jacaranda

flesh unfolds like cloth   I am beginning & ending
                                     destruction & creation

dark & undrained   my oiled hair undoes
                                       7 daggers inside me

where there is nothing and we have not broken in two

Ready

1 Wash your hands please!
She says this as I kick the dirt from my shoes outside.
She is at the stove. I step over the threshold and go to the toilet.
I take off my day clothes and go back to the kitchen. She is
already dishing dhal and herbs on my rice. I sit and watch her
move over to her seat at the kitchen table. We bow our heads
and she says grace. I repeat her amen and hurry to eat.
She does not ask me about my day. When we finish
she clears the plates and I go outside for a smoke.
She would be going to the room now.

I spend a little time staring through the door remembering
the first night we stayed in this house and she slept curled
on the kitchen floor. I go inside and find her
under the bed sheet. Ready and silent. I undress and join her.
She does not move when I push my way inside of her
and slowly begin. She only puts her hands on my shoulders
when I have to go faster. I want this to be over. For her.
For me? She makes me stay inside her after I finish.
To be sure that a child is made. I stare down at her
closed eyes in prayer asking Our Lady to bless us with a boy.
I love her eyelashes and the way her mouth
moves slightly to match the words she is thinking.

2 I told our priest that I was ready
I told her parents these were my intentions
I told my sister's children that she was their new auntie
I cried in bed when it was too late for anyone to be awake
I told myself
I was a man
I was a man

I was a man
I got up and walked to the door
I went back to the bed
I knelt and continued to say the rosary

Lines

howl between C A N E

wash the dhall

boil the water

thick black smoke

close the door properly

light outside moon

wash the rice

salt more salt

iron shakes wind

blind is N I G H T N E S S

Fried Fish

you clean the fish outside
careful not to wet the ground with its innards
you are particular in slicing equal pieces of shad
you even find fish roe
my favourite
slowly removing the sac for chutney
I rub the pieces with ginger and garlic
coat them with masala and salt
thicker you say put more
oil spits back when I throw in the fish
                    we both cough
masala catching our throats

Angel

you call me Angel
you call me bitch when I grab your cock
you call me serious trouble
you call me into your hut at night
you call my name all night long
you call me thief
you call me grass widow
you call me immoral
you call me madrasi
you call me dark
you call me greedy when I ask for my rations
you call me untoward
you call me liar
you call me sinner
you call me christian
you call me pig and dirty beast!
you call me coolie
you call me woman who cried wolf
but I am the wolf itself

Bunny Chow

after we slept in the same bed for a month
we go to your favourite tea-room for a bunny
you wait in line while I keep our seats
I tell three people that the seat opposite is for you
you arrive with two spilling quarter loaves
we eat in silence   and
I watch gravy drip down your hands
this is my first time I say

CHANDANIE SOMWARU

My Language was Found on the Edge of a Mountainside मेरी भाषा एक पहाड़ पर मिली थी

I've been so reckless

अपनी भाषा से इतनी अविचारी हो जाती हूँ

with language that it becomes
a pathway towards

a cliff.

कि यह चट्टान की ओर जाने का रास्ता बन जाती है।

On good days, I call out

किसी अच्छे दिन मैं

hoping language would

बोल उठती हूँ, इस आशा में

bring rocks and pile

कि मेरी भाषा अपने ईंट-पत्थरों को जुगाड़ कर

the rubble
of my tongue

into a bridge एक पुल बना देगी

or gather

या पर्यायी शब्दों का पर्वत अपने हाथों में

a mountain of synonyms

in its hand to place

इकट्ठा कर के

in my mouth.
मेरे मुँह में डाल

देगी।

As a child बचपन में

I would hear main tumhe shaap deta hoon!

And I would
मैं सुनती थी "मैं तुम्हें शाप देता हूँ !" thunder

और मैं ज़ोर से गरजती थी

s
शाप h
a
a
p

picking up

the word's barbed wire and wrapping it around

myself until

अपने शब्दों के काँटेदार तार

को उठा कर अपनी चारों ओर

लपेट कर

I
was

blistered in my own

curse.

तबतक

जबतक

मेरे शरीर पर मेरे शाप के छाले पड़ जाएँ।

I sing *chala gaya*

मैं गाती हूँ

and *charan sharan hum*

aae tumhare

चला गया और चरण शरण हम आए तुम्हारे

not knowing who was going

बिना यह जाने कि कौन जा रहा है

or who I was trying

to come back to.

या मैं किसके पास वापस आने की
कोशिश कर रही हूँ।

I tie the words together   into ropes

of sound

without meaning.

मैं शब्दों को अर्थहीन आवाज़ की रस्सियों में बाँध देती हूँ

My father is too old

मेरे पिताजी अब बूढ़े हो चुके हैं

to teach me what little

जो कुछ उन्हें याद है

मुझे नहीं सिखा पाते

he remembers   but sometimes

his lungs rattle   suno

before the exhale   stales.

कभी उनका सीना खड़खड़ाता है, "सुनो," साँस फीकी पड़ने से पहले ।

To live
बीच-ओ-बीच रहना

in-between—

I only know that every word

my mother knows   my father calls

it

feral.
मैं सिर्फ़ इतना जानती हूँ
कि मेरी माँ के हर एक
शब्द को
मेरे पिताजी
जंगली
कहते हैं।

I check मैं माई की साड़ियों की किनारें ऐसे जाँचती हूँ

the linings of Mai's

saris as if she
were hiding

जैसे वह अपने टाँके में शब्द छिपा रही हो।

words in her stitches.

I ask मैं पूछती हूँ

who has spare

language to throw into
my cup?

क्या किसी के पास थोड़ी
भाषा बाक़ी है, जो वह मेरे प्याले में
फेंक सकते हैं?

Just so I can hear it
rattle
its metal cage

before silence.

ताकि मैं उसके धातु के पिंजरे में उसकी खड़खड़ाहट सुन सकूँ, सन्नाटे से पहले।

I sing
mourning songs

मैं विलाप
के गीत गाती हूँ
अपनी भाषा
के लिए।

for my language.

I offer
language water

and till to quench
its thirst.

मैं अपनी भाषा को पानी और तिल देती हूँ

उसकी प्यास
बुझाने के लिए।

I skin

my

ac

c

ent

मैं अपने उच्चारण को छीलती हूँ

marinate it

in burnt sugar.

और उसे जली हुई शक्कर के सिरके में डालती हूँ।

I am waiting

for the day

मैं उस दिन का इंतजार कर रही हूँ

language reincarnates
into a rooster

जब भाषा मेरी खिड़की के बाहर मुर्गे के रूप में पुनर्जन्म लेगी

outside my window

screaming

और मुझे जगाने के लिए चिल्लाएगी।

for me to wake up.

परदेसी हमारी कहानी लेना चाहता है *Foreigners Want to Take Our Story*

मुँह खोलो!

Open your mouth.

मेरा दुख मुझे वहाँ रखने दो ।

Let me place my sadness there.

माँ, वे सिर्फ़ मेरे आँसुओं पर जीना चाहते हैं ।

Ma, they only want to feed on my tears.

वे नहीं देखना चाहते हमने कैसे अपनी छोटी उँगलियों पर पर्वतों को उठाना सीखा।

They don't want to see how we learned to lift
mountains with our pinkies.

वे नहीं देखना चाहते हम कैसे हवाओं को आवाज़ देते हैं, हमें समुन्दर के पार ले जाने
के मलए।

They don't want to see how we call the wind
to carry us across the ocean.

वे नहीं देखना चाहते हम कैसे नाचते रहते हैं, कैसे अपनी साँसों को बाँसुरी की धुन में
बदलते रहते हैं।

They don't want to see how we keep dancing, how we keep turning
our breath into flute melodies.

तुम कौन होते हो सिर्फ़ दर्द देखनेवाले?

Who are you to want to see the pain?

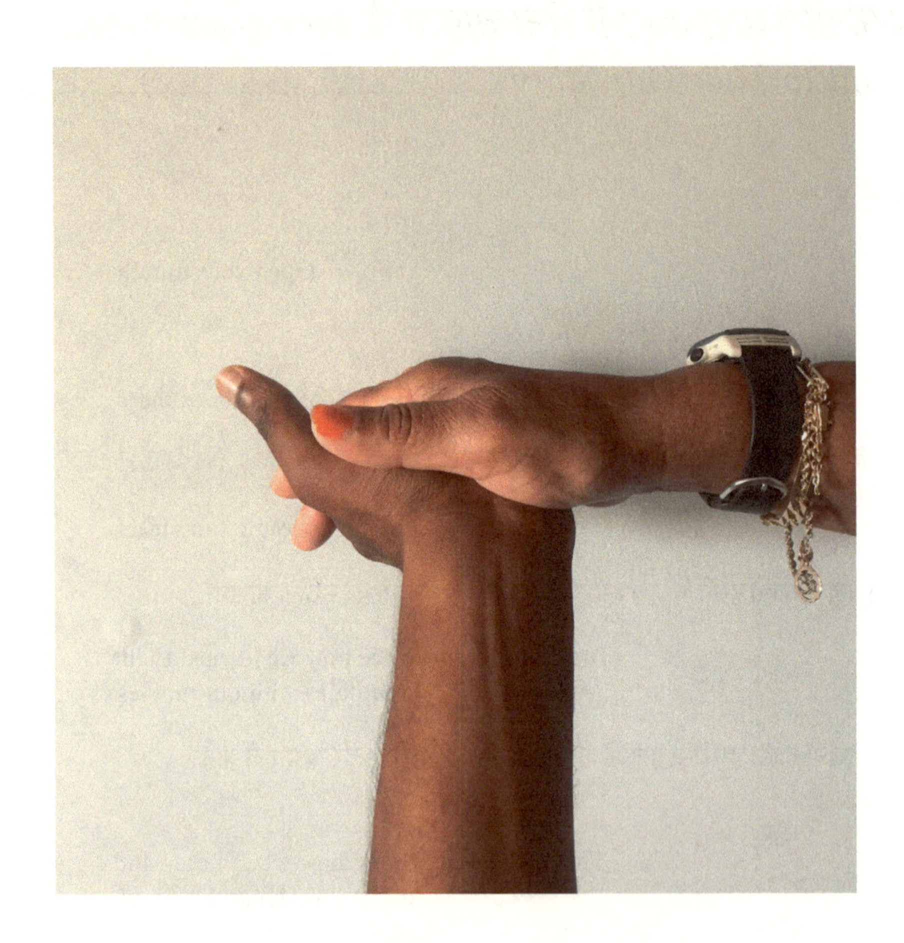

Photograph by Andil Gosine

NICHOLAS AUGUSTUS PETERS

Aloo Gold

In the churning of
Kahari stew
Arose aloo gold
By the hands of
Generations passed.

His thumbs trace
Their way through
Oceans of bargained lies
To arrive on a land
Thought to be a myth.

Circles of charas
Become fields of cutlass
Labouring bitterly for
A sweetness that kills from
Root to liver to consciousness.

But chattri hands
Were made for battle
With palms designed to
Caress the seedlings
Of his love.

And, with the fingers
Of kin, they stir
Baby-pots of
A new black water
Brew.

WILL DEPOO

Voices from the Kalapani

Tassa playing hard
Palms moving fast on deh tabla
Singer on deh harmonium
Dem voice filled with Bhojpuri
Meh nah undastand
But I hear cries from the plantation
Oh lawd, dem trick abi
Voices holding onto language
Instruments holding onto culture
Now we get glimpses of this
Aunties ah mek same cries at religious functions
Are they hoping Bihar will hear dem?

Coolie Nightmare

Tears rolling down his body
Sinking into the kalapani
Hoping it'll reach Mother Ganga
Hoping lawd will tell the ancestors
Nah fuh come
Blood deh pon di cutlass
Limbs amongst deh paddies
El Dorado nah gold
Ee ah brecka drink fuh control abi
Mek abi mad
Your sons, and their sons, and their sons will carry this
Some will try to erase or drain the blood, the DNA
They will carry the memories of the slaughter

Guyana Independence, Guyana Sentence

Dem force abi come ah this land
Capture abi from West Africa
Trick abi from Asia
Cut cane fuh brecka
Abi fight back
Brecka send he army
Send missionaries fuh trick we
Seh liqa ah mek abi feel better
Abi rebel
Brecka wan war
Divide and rule dem strategy
Abi agi and nani face the brunt
Ah home, outside, in foreign
Dem seh abi free now
How we free wen estate close, can't fish
Abi ah come backtrack
Wuk fuh pennies
Abi fuhget Rodney
Abi fuhget fuh fight

Crimmigration Story

real cold night pon Liberty
ganja ah bun
"family" playing as dropped g37 pass by
babylon pull up
ah question dem dis
ee seh pull out id
one ah dem nah get id
ee nah get papers
babylon ask where is the weed
queens da wan fill queens county
dem gee he back
babylon put deh cold metal pon dem hand
"wah abi do!" dem seh
is this a marijuana cigarette on the ground
babylon reaching into dem pocket
mayor seh abi nah fuh get arrested fuh ganja
it's up to the boro smart asses babylon responds
dem spend night ah bookings
one day, he got a letter from dhs
says come two weeks review status
wah me gon do ee seh
lawyer want 10,000 fuh walk with meh
construction nah pay suh, bossman nah pay 3 weeks
baby need formula
if meh nah go, dem gon come fuh meh
goes to the "check-in" alone
dem seh can't leave
going to Hudson
family pay 10,000
lawyer never go court
judge seh ee must gan
lawyer want 15,000
10,000 all dem save
ee gan

Babylon Gwan Fall

Babylon ah come in different forms
White supremacists in the form of patriots
Assaulters selected to deh highest court
Dehumanizing abi
Calling abi criminals or illegals
Locking we in cages
Deporting abi fuh dead
Babylon gwan fall
People nah tek dis sufferation
Abi gon follow deh Dalit mantra
Educate, agitate and organize
Babylon gwan fall
The day fuh come when
Collective ah win
Violence against pickney and woman gone
Babylon nah patrol, nah murder abi
Abi ah keep matti safe
No one in cages
Border nah deh
Babylon gwan fall

GITAN DJELI

iel.and

specks of land craters grumbled from ocean floors
eight million years igneous rocks ancient polyps red
mangroves

mantle home to ground-dwelling unwinged bipeds
seacows keel-scaled boas wedgetailed shearwaters and
giant parakeets

isle/land named renamed unnamed man-named dotted
by maps

archipelago   of   lands

flattened framed from settler orientation extraction
subtraction where life ogled of its last breath from a
fraction of a grid topography

the blue mountains have witnessed they remember
they murmur the story of geography

djinn

our aunts not only tell us to learn lesson and survive they teach us to
confide care and unhaunt they tell us on such nights to
release dreamare apparitions we remember and retell them
before midday to someone we love

the act of conjuring together form a ritual of salt and spit to
split images and spirits into speech and words is
to speak with and away they see her leave the room we
look around she moves the device

and here it is la dame blanche on the polystyrene cornice in
the ceiling of the room who shifts to the camera her eye the
size of a lens on which her finger turns the screen flesh
orange they hear her nine thousand

kilometres away she screams of her aunt who we incensed
the previous day with opium sticks dried petals and
ancestral blood the aunt like the mother whose curse to the
lover who killed her we know is irretrievable

they emerge from lips of southern seas

ore oru oorile

a long time ago in that place three
messengers floated on the docks until they
lock spirits in the soil a kalimaye grew from
the earth and lores of two continents and
three oceans seeded

to suck the sugar poison sisters placed seven
stones under a banyan tree for there were no
neem they spread cockerel blood sindoor
candles and lamps to rally women and revel
in the colours of tree root herstorytelling and
evening baithkās

to teach in kreol tamoul bojpouri old tongues
and new tongues from ancestral lines

usulu: planet in emakhuwa

she asks to imagine stories in tongues of ancestors from lands
continents stories that do not discover voyage arrive and
settle

sea currents unsettle flow ripple wind as planets rotate
and radiate the ocean gyre and swirl from indonesian
archipelagoes to the african sea and brush against cliffs of
the kreol isles spiral around madagascan coral reefs and
sweep shoals of mozambique the spirits do the same they
continue to gather roam and guide   an ancient story
circulates

on the shores of moma that seapeople across times have
followed the movements of the great salty lake and
travelled to the islands twelve families sustained by the
ocean today retell how lost at sea currents returned them
to the continent to the same coastline where captured
emakhuwa ancestors rebelled on ships sang and danced
tufu from which they composed sega

for nations people have followed rhymes of planets and
moons and tides and sea currents and ocean lands

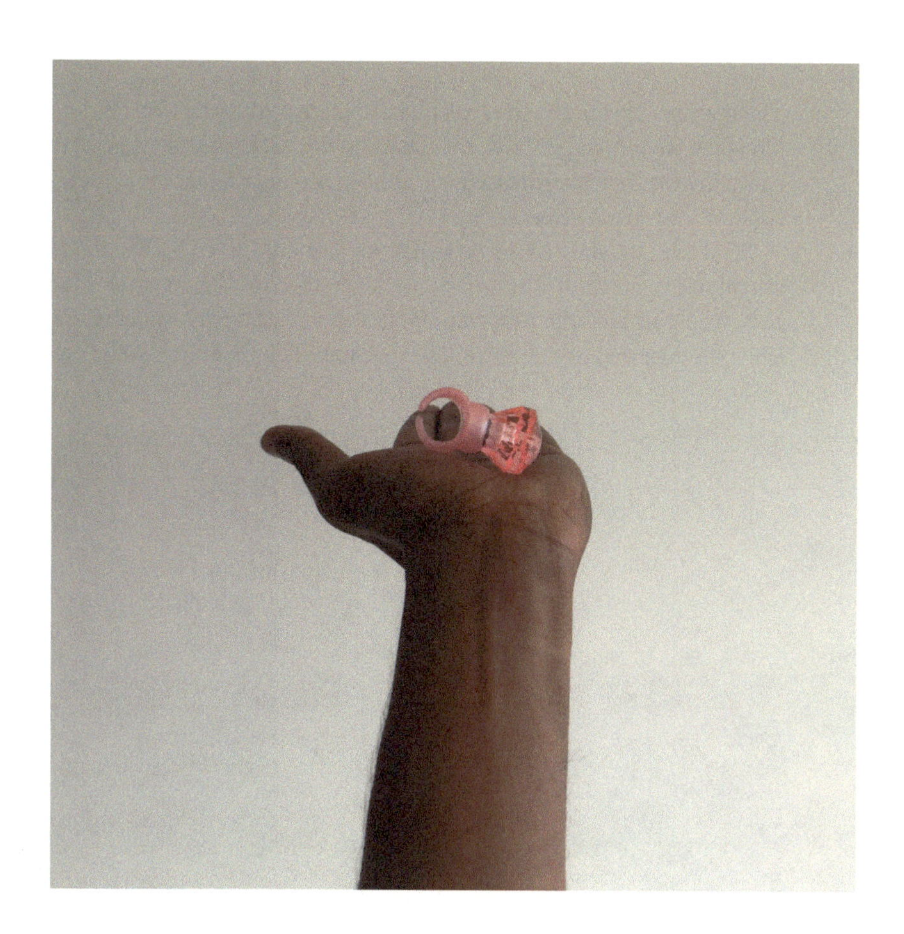

Photograph by Andil Gosine

Rising

The men eat upstairs in the Executive Lounge of the Marriott. We stay there too when we return. MSNBC drones on in the background. Most of them, oil company workers overdressed and sunburned in this place that hangs off the equator, are from Texas.

My father, the son of a Cornelia-Ida rice farmer, worked his first job pumping gas in Georgetown to afford math textbooks for his A-level exams. His boss, who managed the Esso station back then, asked *why would you leave this* when he migrated to the Bahamas. That was code for *you're better off settling.*

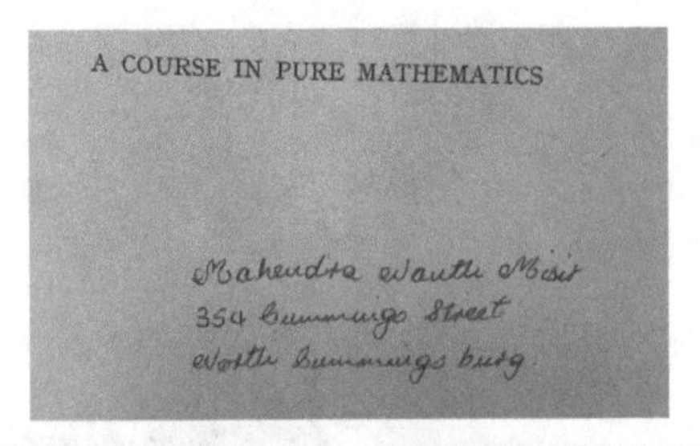

A COURSE IN PURE MATHEMATICS

Mahendra Nauth Misir
354 Cummings Street
North Cummingsburg

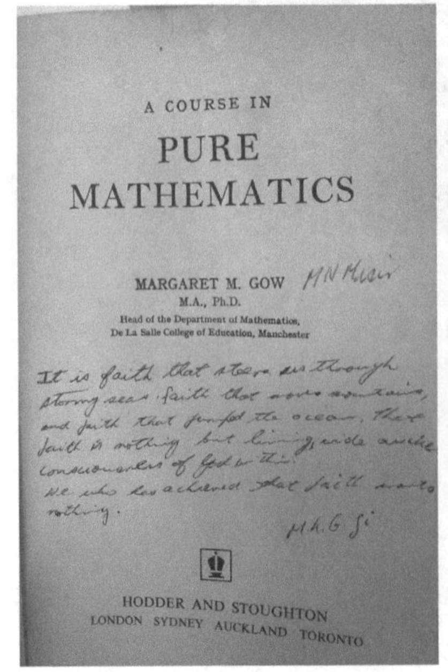

A COURSE IN

PURE MATHEMATICS

MARGARET M. GOW
M.A., Ph.D.
Head of the Department of Mathematics,
De La Salle College of Education, Manchester

HODDER AND STOUGHTON
LONDON SYDNEY AUCKLAND TORONTO

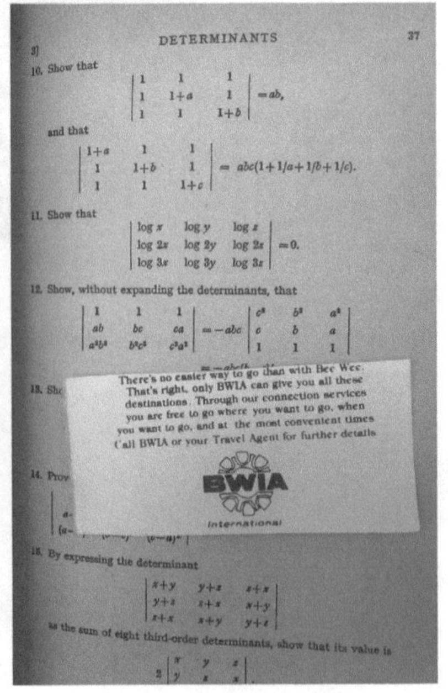

DETERMINANTS 37

3]

10. Show that

$$\begin{vmatrix} 1 & 1 & 1 \\ 1 & 1+a & 1 \\ 1 & 1 & 1+b \end{vmatrix} = ab,$$

and that

$$\begin{vmatrix} 1+a & 1 & 1 \\ 1 & 1+b & 1 \\ 1 & 1 & 1+c \end{vmatrix} = abc(1+1/a+1/b+1/c).$$

11. Show that

$$\begin{vmatrix} \log x & \log y & \log z \\ \log 2x & \log 2y & \log 2z \\ \log 3x & \log 3y & \log 3z \end{vmatrix} = 0.$$

12. Show, without expanding the determinants, that

$$\begin{vmatrix} 1 & 1 & 1 \\ ab & bc & ca \\ a^2b^2 & b^2c^2 & c^2a^2 \end{vmatrix} = -abc \begin{vmatrix} c^2 & b^2 & a^2 \\ c & b & a \\ 1 & 1 & 1 \end{vmatrix}$$

13. Sh

14. Prov

15. By expressing the determinant

$$\begin{vmatrix} x+y & y+z & z+x \\ y+z & z+x & x+y \\ z+x & x+y & y+z \end{vmatrix}$$

as the sum of eight third-order determinants, show that its value is

We eat outside on the balcony of the lounge one night, and it made me feel seasick. To return is a privilege. To stay here is a privilege. To wax poetic about diaspora from a distance is a privilege. *do you even understand what was lost to bring you here*, Safia Elhillo writes in "to make use of water."

My father's first chore as a child was to chase the birds from the rice fields. He recounts a memory of taking hundreds of eggs to Leonora Market in a basket to sell when he was eight years old. He works in IT now and is comfortably middle-class, but he always returns to the rice fields of his youth when the color of a shirt in his closet rings his memory like a bell. He taught me how to tip well because labor is more than work.

The air con inside the lounge is trash compared to the sea breeze that rolls in from the brown water of the Demerara River. Or is it the Atlantic? At some point, the mouth of the river unfurls into the ocean. Dad points out where both meet, but it's all just water to me. He notes GuyBridge to the left, the fourth-longest floating bridge in the world, that connects Georgetown to West Bank Demerara. It's kept afloat by 114 pontoons.

I'm constantly confused by the difference between East Bank, East Coast, and West Bank, West Coast. The language of where water meets land guides how people understand geography here. You can be on the bank of a river or on the coast of the Atlantic. I get the banks and coasts wrong on the first draft. "Just look at the map, Nad," my dad says. But even then, it's all just water to me.

When we drive over GuyBridge the next morning, it feels like we are dangerously close to the water. I become hyperaware of our proximity to water when we return to Guyana three times after my grandparents die. In New York, I'm used to bridges that tower above currents, not comfortably skim the top of them. I'm used to bridges carrying trains between boroughs and to the rumble of the J train hustling over the Williamsburg Bridge.

On that day on the lounge's balcony, Mom recounts taking walks across GuyBridge when she was a teenager. Bamboo sticks with colorful flags tied to them dot the shore below, markers of where morning prayers were offered to the water. We note how much sky there is here.

What was never there before: an oil rig, floating like a period with no sentence in the distance.

Exxon's webpage declares that the corporation is now "firmly established in Guyana."

***

God said to Noah: *Seven days from now I will send rain on the earth for forty days and forty nights, and I will wipe from the face of the earth every living creature I have made.*

It is a precise punishment, one defined by numbers. Noah is 600 years old on the "seventeenth day of the second month" when the floodwaters arrive, and the rain did fall for 40 days and 40 nights. Mountains are submerged more than 20-feet underwater and the floodwaters remain for 150 days.

"Georgetown gon' sink. We have plenty life jacket ready. You don' worry. We gon head into di Interior when it happen," Sister Lynn, the herbalist who has been living in my grandparents' home since they migrated out, tells my mom with a conviction I envy. I, too, want to have unwavering faith in something. This time, Sister Lynn warns, we should listen to the Lord.

The Union of Concerned Scientists, according to their Twitter, "puts rigorous, independent science to work to solve our planet's most pressing problems." Their Climate Hot Map is dedicated to showing how global warming is affecting the world now.

The observation that "without improved sea and river defenses and drainage systems, the coastal plains of coastal Guyana face serious flooding—if not complete inundation" is a devastating one. Not just because parts of Guyana's coast already "sit from 19.7 to 39.4 inches below sea level," but because 80 percent of the population lives in those coastal parts. Protections that are in place: seawalls, mangroves, and natural sandbanks.

***

For a country whose coast already suffers from erosion and mangroves that are dying off as sea levels rise, oil drilling and production are a kind of death sentence.

The Nandy Park house stands on stilts high enough that we call the space below the first floor the bottom house. Sister Lynn sees her patients here. I imagine the flood water rising up, the clinic submerged, waves overtaking the verandah, and patients floating in orange life jackets. It is easy for me to accept Lynn's sermon as hyperbole and to laugh at the absurdity of it and her fierce belief in verses of the Bible.

Guyana is covered in water, but it's not submerged. Yet.

When I hear the word *rise*, I think slow, calculated, and rising up from the wooden pews of a church with its feet firmly planted in the earth. The sea is doing something more than just rising. It is soaring. Leaping. Revolting.

dear nandy park house

that rests on wooden stilts   that assumes

floodwater

that birthed the bottomhouse sleeping

beneath our feet   house that swells and creaks with the rain

like an inflamed joint

house with iron grillwork spread like a

bedsheet

over mom's bedroom window

old house with the window that frames the goosebery tree outside

will you walk on water?

They call it first oil. The date and time of birth are recorded. December 20, 2019, 9:34 p.m. Sagittarius sun, Libra moon, Leo rising. The headline:

"'It meant so much to me' … EBD youth says on being the first to test Guyana's oil."

The misguided optimism is not an exception, despite the fact that the first oil came without "necessary systems like a local content policy or a petroleum commission." "Bittersweet," the *Guyana Times International* calls it.

We record the dates of things like disasters. December 20, 2019 is no different.

Photographs by author.

C. GOVENDER

Fermentation

Bruised mangoes beach on sorrows of sugar,
searching for unbleached rainbows of sugar.

Bent folk chant in a sickle paradise,
bathed in flickering lamp glows of sugar.

Mothers, fathers bound by a single cross,
the die cast for boundless throws of sugar.

Even fishing lines arc towards the sun.
Arrows don't return to bows of sugar.

Barracks become homes with garland thresholds;
mudras unfold in meadows of sugar.

Oh, the sweet balm of Lata and Asha!
Quiet escape in pillows of sugar.

Cheers for Dhoni, Dravid and de Villiers!
Boundaries cracked from willows of sugar!

Dung beetles roam free. What if you waited,
but there were no tomorrows of sugar?

After the flames, a residue lingers.
Roots ember in the shadows of sugar.

How to count the plural that's Natal, our
Lost-and-Founds in these plateaus of sugar?

Augna

50 sheep to look after
one did not return

the boy stayed away
fear

the missing sheep the boy
return

Mr. Meikle tied the boy's hands
hung him naked
to a rafter in the dining-room
thrashed him
with a hunting crop

hanging for an hour
two feet
from the ground

when breakfast came
sent off with the sheep

the other Coolies witnessed
my son being beaten

one of my sons
Augna (25980)
about 10 years of age
left the estate

never returned

could not be found

has not been heard of since

Composed using fragments from a found text: testimony of Bhagoo to the Protector of Indian Immigrants dated February 19, 1884 (I.I./1/18, 18911884, Natal Archives) in *A Documentary History of Indian South Africans 1860 - 1982*, eds. Surendra Bhana and Bridglal Pachai, in association with the Centre for Intergroup Studies, Cape Town, South Africa (Cape Town and Johannesburg: David Philip, Publisher and Stanford, California: Hoover Institution Press, 1984), 5, from South African History Online, www.sahistory.org.za/archive/4-complaint-ill-treatment-estate (accessed: December 04, 2023).

Exit Signs

I

Addicted to drinking,
but he had got over that.

He showed unmistakable signs
of insanity for a few weeks

before he made away
with himself.

II

A fairly well-nourished man
about 35 years of age,
always been peculiar.

A man of ungovernable temper,
melancholy and snappish in the interval

but a good workman.

His wife died 12 months ago.
He has since lived alone.

He had his head shaved on Sunday,
a significant act.

On Monday, he was very thirsty.

Mr. McEwan called upon me to say
a Coolie of his was dead.

The Indian Ramaiya no. 22128
committed suicide.

The noose was artistically made.

Composed using fragments from found texts: Medical and employer reports on the death of Ramaiya (I.I./1/21, 119511884, Natal Archives) in *A Documentary History of Indian South Africans 1860 - 1982*, eds. Surendra Bhana and Bridglal Pachai, in association with the Centre for Intergroup Studies, Cape Town, South Africa (Cape Town and Johannesburg: David Philip, Publisher and Stanford, California: Hoover Institution Press, 1984), 17, from South African History Online, www.sahistory.org.za/archive/14-suicide-among-indentured-labourers (accessed: December 04, 2023).

Sugar and Spice and All Things Nice

Manicured beds betray her green fingers.
Anthuriums cared for by sateen fingers.

Tender *camellia sinensis* tips
just clipped in a flutter of keen fingers.

Hitched saris crochet across Kearsney's slopes
—a Future shaped by unforeseen fingers.

As you steep and strain leaves—oxidised black—
whispers remain, can stain silkscreen fingers.

What games were they playing when dowries came?
And what did their eyes say, smokescreen fingers?

Prices paid. Sacrifices will be made.
How do we value tourmaline fingers?

The spectrum was binary: White. Not White.
No light could define In-Between-Fingers.

Tongaat-Hulett filed for business rescue—
unceremonious end, unclean fingers?

Yet the days still begin with tea rituals,
and tamarind seeds rinsed with lean fingers.

That's what Ayahs are made of. Salt and bark
and sheer watermark and Unseen Fingers.

Month-End Morning in a Kwa-Zulu Natal Town

Someone must have placed funeral homes
among flamboyants and internet cafés
in the town at the end of the hills.
Faux flowers, coffins with ornate handles and wily undertakers
greet shoppers buying staples on Osborne Road.
But they don't pause to say hello.

Someone must have snatched their time and smiles
with their jobs and their families
when HIV AIDs and the recession came
and stayed, when sugar spot prices remained low.

They walk right past,
the gait of people whose cards are dealt,
KFC and Steers bulging in the lush
forest canopies, cane fields and birdsong.

Someone must be hungry
in this town once graced
by Queen Elizabeth and her family,
resting place of Nandi, mother of Shaka, the Zulu King,
still on the birders' map.

SHIVANEE RAMLOCHAN

Plumeria

Mother,
when they opened my penis
they found flowers

Frangipani petals flickered
underneath the foreskin
petals as wet as a river

When the line between
boy and country of origin
starts to bleed, I crumple in
moth time, all the wings of

My body, furring in the dark
Mother, did you know the
knife of the schoolyard bully
and the surgeon's scalpel

Sing out with a same sharpness?

Remember the time you found me
my ankles guilty in your shoes
and you chased me through the house
belt raised with rainy season choking
the wind, not a one of us in tears
while you did what you needed
to my ankles, turned them

From flowers to crosses leaking blood

Catechism

I built my language in the territory of dykes
Brave baby lesbian of the after-school choir
practice, convent uniform skirt higher than
a soprano's quaver, fingered in the sacristy

I unfrotted religion between the warmth I
understood (all island, all holy, all wrong to
the touch) and the heat I invented (the place
beneath my bed filled with cavernous porns)

I've come by this the hard way, on my elbows
scrubbing the lines of scripture out my tongue
Floored by priests' knees between recesses, a
shallow learner of their psaltery and sexual bribe

You think it was a man's touch that turned me gay
Though it might be easier, Father, to give the
Sunday school of rapes the credit for what wrong
wombed woman I have made myself, the truth is

You, building me in the soft yolk of your teenage
years, knew without knowing the thing I would
become: where I started, ball of mucus and star
skin and pus, I was your child, dyking the firmament

You cannot imagine all the gayness I have undone
to teach myself to be someone like your son.

Fulminant

Like lightning / forking through /your suprasternal notch

Like your aji's voice / brassy and suspicious

if you eh train the boy / he go rotten / he go spoil

Like when you left
the hospital and for days
the sound of a light switch
made you piss a little

Like the first time
following deconversion
When her tongue slid into
your mouth and you're so

Sorry but it tasted like death
Like sucking on the cylinder
Of the exhaust pipe those boys
Beat your head against when
You were nine, hammering your
Fine bones into a fuselage, like
This is what it means to feel
Like you're going to die, oh
Okay that's it, I'm going to
Die, okay that's it I'm deading now

Like. All right. This is what you'd
say when asked, when the therapist
Pushes her ballpoint nib gentle
In the centre of her stenopad and
Asks, like there is an answer

What, can you tell me, in your
Own words and please, take your time
What did it feel like when they
Held you down and applied the
Volts like shots like love cracked
Down the cistern like a bowl
Broken into china parts for dolls
With no fucking heads or guts

Novena for a Lover, Beaten to Death

Let the whole island know
I ran naked after the donkey cart they
used for a hearse. Blood orchids
sprung under my feet as I chased him, bawling

for the body on that
packbeast, velveteen-eared
holding my virginity in its blue palms
like a sprawling moth.

Beyond the church where I am not bid
I shall throw my ribs open to the sea.
For it may be possible, even after death
for an Adam to beget another Adam from love.

If it were not love I would beg the island
to stone me for the shame of it. Let
every coconut tree massacre my skull
with fruit. Let the brown skin crack as milk.

When I was fifteen, I held the penis of the man
now dead in my mouth like a sacrament, his fifteen
year old heart beating so fast under the school
stairwell, my wet prick in my hand, budding seed.

No one would show me the autopsy,
yet I imagine his brain butterflied under the sky
at night. I imagine the ropes of his slack ribs fluttering
goodbye when the body was licked good morning

by dogs

Mother, there was a time when I laid my
head in your hands, felt your fingers rush over
my ears as water does from our highest rocks.
How you whispered to me that I was holy, knit well

Our Father, his father, and mine, please know
I have tried to be a good son.
Hear me howling these nine nights outside the tomb,
my body a vestment for your knives.

Photograph by Andil Gosine

N. NARDINA BI

My Big Aunty Karahee: Five Lyric Meditations

DICTIONARY KARAHEE

(Creolese; Guyanese Creole)
Karahee; Karahi | kuh-raa-hee; /kə.ˈrɑː.hiː/

Noun:

1. A pot used for cooking stew, curry, and rice and for frying, amongst other things

**See also*
Kaharee; Kahari | kuh-haa-ree; /kə.ˈhɑː.riː/
Noun:

1. A current Georgetown pronunciation of "karahee"/"karahi"

    which I learned in Canada from my dear Town sibling after
    I first saw GT

(English)
Karahee; Karahi | kuh-ra-hee; /kə.ˈrɑː.ɦiː/
Noun:

1. A deep pot of various sizes and diameters of South Asian origin in style and similar to a wok, often made of aluminum or iron and frequently used for stews, cooking rice, frying, etc.

the tongues they lost, new versions I studied
lek how dem ol' bound people bina taakk, sirka 1870
but not quite the same as modern Urdu and Hindi

(Hindustani; Urdu-Hindi; Hindi-Urdu)
کڑھاہی; कढ़ाही | trans. kaṛāhī; kadai | /kə.ɽɑː.ɦiː/
Noun, feminine:

1. A two-handled cooking vessel with deep/slanted sides used for frying
2. A dish cooked in a kaṛāhī

PHONETIC KARAHEE

Kuh-raa-hee. The "ka" is short with an "uh," and the "raa" and "hee" are sung with long vowels. Our creole calypso calls out all the consonants, but across the Caribbean Sea in North America, WASP English teaches us to swallow the middle syllable "ra" and slightly eat the H in the "hee." The "ra" is American, like in

"**r**eminde**r**"

of the "**r**obbing" of our "fa**r**-**r**emoved" "**r**elatives"

from which something new was "**r**eborn"

and from which we continue to "**r**ecove**r**,"

"**r**ecognize,"

and "**r**ediscove**r**."

Here in North America, or maybe for others it is imperial Europe, is where coolie sounds, coolie tastes, coolie looks, coolie history, coolie existence, and coolie being meet and confront the non-coolie South Asian and modes of "Indianness" untouched by indenture and never translated into something new and irreversible. These are the loci where our karahee meet the kadai, and everything is unfamiliar yet vaguely familiar. Indentured scars and wounds of missing an imagined home a century or more away, some even idealize. I ask you: is that India home to a karahee full of cookup with a little of everything Guyanese? Our Dougla karahee? Our Black karahee? Our Indigenous karahee? Our Chinese karahee? Our mixed-race karahee? Our karahee from the cane fields, where castes blended together and were forever forgotten?

From karahee to kadai, everything is swallowed. The "*kuh*" down to the "*ra*" and the "*hee.*" The "*ra*" is not replaced, but sometimes written with a D, a sound the British could not fit into twenty-six letters. The air-sung retroflex R is a dance of singular contraction that our tongues do not know in Guyana. And even the H is almost silent and invisible, like the knowledge of indenture and where Guyana sits on the map, one cheek kissing the Caribbean and the other kissing South America.

GREETING KARAHEE

Every time I would visit my aunties, my shoes were barely off my feet, and I was still washing my hands when they'd command, "come, come nah and eat!" Even if I had just eaten or didn't want to eat, there was no saying "no." There was always a big silver pot of food on the stove. And sometimes there were several pots. The aluminum cauldrons had bellies 14" to 20" in diameter, and these were tools all my Guyanese aunties kept in their cabinets and ovens when not in use. No matter whose house it was, they all had the same pots with rounded sides, not quite rough but not quite smooth either, and squarish, rectangular handles. The lids had a little black button knob that was prone to getting too hot when boiling away. Every pot was etched with the uppercase letters reading "IMUSA," but the aunties always called them "karahee." And, on special occasions or you were just at the right aunty's house, she'd take out that old Guyana karahee with the round bottom that came here in a suitcase years ago. It was either black iron or silver aluminum, and the curved sides weren't so steep like the IMUSA cauldron's, and the handles were little circles standing upright like Winnie-the-Pooh's ears. But these were smaller and couldn't carry the full capacity of the IMUSA giants.

Holding my aunty's hand walking down the tall steps from the four-train platform standing high above Jerome Avenue in the Bronx after school or after a long, weekend car ride in traffic to the other corner of the city in Queens, at Big Aunty's, Middle Aunty's, or even my uncles', there was always a karahee exerting a strong aroma of spices from a warm and rich gravy, something I knew I would scoop up with white rice or provisions like green or sweet plantains, starchy cassava, little eddoes, and yams in a spoon or between my fingers with roti or bake. Sometimes on a special occasion and there was money left over, cousins, aunties, and uncles would take over three or four tables in Delhi Palace in Jackson Heights, Queens, or Curry in a Hurry on Lexington Avenue in Manhattan, and, on the menu, there was a "kadai" we didn't know and didn't order. We thought it was a hard, dental D. But all of the food, none the less delicious, was cooked in karahees in a kitchen in the back in ways we didn't know and served in little stainless steel and copper buckets that looked like little karahees.

"Dis how real cooliemon, real Indiyamon food a taste," the old people dem would say, even if they weren't coolies like us.

When I was barely able to see over the kitchen counter, my little eyes gazed up to the stovetop, and seeing the big silver pot wide and sturdy above, I knew they were ancient and older than me. Every aunty's karahee carried stories of its own and knew their hands from the time they first came to New York in the '70s and '80s, from when they first lived on the Grand Concourse and bought those IMUSA pots. These karahees fed five people living in a studio or one-bedroom apartment in the early years, and they were carried in and out of doors, down steps, in precarious elevators with accordion gate doors, on the subway, and in cars to family functions, at any time possibly surpassing 20 lbs. in weight to feed the mouths of twenty or thirty people or more.

My aunties' karahees brought us all the tastes of a country they and the old people dem were too afraid to return to, and one they taught me I could never visit. Any curry coming out of their karahees would put a spell on me as a piknee. Though, their favorite curry was one I couldn't belly and one that still scares me even as an adult. Walking into their apartment through the door, Daddy loved hearing them call out "mi juss make hassar curry."

The genus of small catfish is enclosed in a shelly exoskeleton. I never saw one in the Museum of Natural History, but it is on display in the Guyana National Museum in Georgetown. While hassar could be found for sale in the freezers of Caribbean supermarkets imported or farmed in South Florida—sometimes under the Trinbagonian name of "cascadoo"—their delicacy was hassar wrapped in newspaper and a plastic bag, previously thawing out in a suitcase after flying from South America. They loved opening the pot and gazing at the hassar simmering whole in the brown gravy, but when it came to hassar, I preferred the karahee with the lid on.

Hassar[1] curry is like any curry:

1. Grease the karahee with a few glugs of oil.
2. Cook your aromatics to get rid of the raw taste.
3. Add your masala and spices, and bring them alive.
4. Add water as necessary, chunkay it real good, and cook it down into a paste.
5. Curry the hassar.

While I was never keen on that fish, as a child I loved going over to my aunties', and first thing I'd wash my hands and watch them fish for a beef or goat bone from the bottom of the karahee they'd make sure to keep just for me. It gave me a certain euphoria to suck out the buttery ambrosia of marrow coated with curry. My nose would sniffle and my lips would tingle from the pepper, and the aunties would giggle seeing a little four-year-old clean off those bones.

[1]The R in "hassar" is silent.

GENDERING AND GENDERED KARAHEE

The karahee is the tool of aunties, just like a tawa,[2] a belna,[3] and a pot spoon. In my childhood, my aunties made every type of curry in their karahee: chicken, duck, beef, goat, lamb, fish, shrimp, crab, pumpkin, aloo, kathahar, mango, channa, squash, and even pachownie. They fried golden pholourie in their karahees, little balls of spicy and garlicy fried split pea batter, and there was an unspoken competition of whose was best and not flour-ie, but real pholourie. They made chicken stew, and, for Christmas, they made pepper pot, our Indigenous dish creolized with triangle-trade chunks of meat simmered in a cinnamon and clove bath with garlic, red chili pepper, and umber cassareep, where cassava and molasses meet and become one.

For Big Eid and Qurbani Eid, my aunties melted ghee in their karahees, bubbling away yellow, in which they toasted white flour with warm, sweet spices and added cans of evaporated milk, condensed milk, raisins, and candied cherries, bright and artificial red, to make the sweet paste of sirnee, prasad, or mohan bog. From the karahee to the ittie, bittie Ziploc bags, their sirnee would disappear, and the karahees would be washed and hidden away behind a door or above the fridge, and you'd never know everything they carried, everything they cooked, and all those hours they labored, never asked, never thanked, just done.

Aunties and their karahees carry us home. Whether it be my aunties from Guyana or someone else's from around the world with a big IMUSA pot lined with pegao or concón, the crispy rice stuck at the bottom, or a pot full of jollof with the grains of rice coated with the concoction of spices, hot and sweet pepper, and tomato. Aunties bring home to home, whether we be far or near, new or long in this place we find home, albeit it isn't where we originally came from. They labor, never asked, never thanked, just done. In the summertime, some aunties would set up their karahees on a burner with a kerosene tank in the driveways on the side of the house at the cookout, and at the beach, they'd set up a fire and slowly feed a log in underneath the karahee over many hours until that duck falls off the bone in the curry. Karahees outside keep the smell of spices, onions, and garlic frying out of the living room and out of the just-folded laundry. Back home, before they had gas stoves and indoor plumbing, the aunties cooked outside, and, here, the old people dem relived a nostalgia for old ways, the simple ways, fireside pon di chulha. They always remembered the science to get the flame just perfect, really, not just a science but an art. But do they remember how the smell of burnt coals and smoke cling to your clothes and hair? Do they remember the drips of sweat pouring down your face as you blow into the

[2] A "tawa" is a griddle used for cooking flatbreads such as roti, dhal puri, and paratha, or oil roti (also known as "buss up shut").

[3] A "belna" means "rolling pin" in Creolese, as introduced from Caribbean Hindustani.

embers to keep them alive while their dust jumps on you and grabs you like Ol' Haigue and the Soukouyant if you're not careful?

***

Before I was born, I imagine my Ajee and Big Aunty back home in countryside Guyana, waking up with the fowl's call to sweat over a karahee. Picture my grandma and my eldest aunty cooking breakfast and lunch for more than a half dozen children, my aunty's siblings and Daddy,—my grandfather, and whoever else is hungry that may come asking for a meal. Imagine doing it again seven days a week before refrigerators made it to their rural home, and all the washing up by hand after. For generations on that plantation, or the one where Daddy was born, or down the coast where Ajee's grandfather was indentured, they used to grow cane tall to process into sugar. Starting as young girls, my aunties' aunties and their aunties and their aunties stood over karahees cooking whatever food they had, often rations from the sugar estate, fish right from boats a short walk away, and provisions from the yard. Still today, the karahees sing with bubbling oil when they fry breadfruit and plantains. The karahees chime with every knock of the spoon after each stir. The bound coolies brought their karahees from India with their spices and their ways of cooking, which we carry along with the same parallel riches and knowledge of what we Guyanese inherited from those enslaved and trafficked from West Africa. We know our cassareep from the Indigenous Peoples of the Land of Many Waters and chow mein and red bean cake from the Chinese who came bound like our ancestors too and those who came not-bound to set up shops. The aunties still sweat over karahees adorned in flowy flower frocks to feed the men and children, though years have passed since aunties were bound on the plantation. How they still labor, never asked, never thanked, just done.

Of my cousins born in the United States, not quite old enough to have been married but old enough to help in the kitchen and feed themselves, I can't say for certain how many know to mix the masala for curry and roll out dough for roti to cook on a tawa. I can't say how many of my cousins—distanced enough from the migration of aunties when they first left Guyana and oldest cousins, now aunties themselves—keep a karahee as their tool. But when I was a piknee, I learned and wanted to learn the magic of the karahee. I wanted to learn the magic of aunties. I wanted to learn the magic of food, mixing this and that and transforming it into something more and something elevated that makes you close your eyes and moan, "mmmmmmmmmmmm." But maybe there was a part of me that thought this is what good girls, obedient girls, girls who don't cause trouble, girls who fit in, and—above all—girls who are liked, do, even though that's something I couldn't fully understand at eight years old. From when I was in diapers, I watched Big Aunty and Middle Aunty in the kitchen. They know just how much of each spice to sprinkle into the pot, never counting with spoons or measuring cups. Middle Aunty would stick her bare hand right above the hot oil to dip in the little balls of pholourie batter or triangles of dough to fry bake, and she didn't even flinch when the oil splashed. I would help and roll out the roti and dhal puri or mix the batter, even when the wiriwiri pepper burned my little hands. I always stood watching. You could say I knew I wanted to be an aunty too.

***

At functions when the family would all come together, the bed sheets lined the floor on which sat the cousins and the aunties and uncles, though the meyjee and his wife always sat on the couch, and the smoke of the argarbatti did its last dance around the living room with a trail of the grey ash leading back to the sherry glass full of uncooked rice grains anchoring the incense sticks that once stood up. The descendants of those carried across the ocean still know to read namaz, a Persian word I learned from my Caribbean kin over a decade before I learned to connect the noun to the mim to the alif and to the ze in a university classroom. The descendants of those carried across the ocean still have jhandis and still sing bhajans before eating seven curry out of a lotus or banana leaf, just like the tales of Mami Wata are not forgotten, nor is Mother Oshun. The aunties gathered in the kitchen to heat up food, and they called the girl cousins in behind them. This was my favorite part of Quran Shareefs as a child: the pure pleasure that came from eating what my aunties cooked in their karahees—food I didn't get every day at home, food mommy didn't know to cook in our Guyanese-Sicilian house where we didn't have a Guyanese aunty living, though Mommy tried and tried hard.

Out would come Afeefa with a pitcher of water and a bowl to catch it fall, and Imani with a towel to dry our hands with which we would eat, no spoons or forks. Zeinab would pass out pholourie and tangy tamarind chutney and the bags of sweet, sweet sirnee we'd begin to devour with rumbling bellies after sitting through the reading of the meyjee's caribbeanified Arabic and his sermon. Melissa would bring out plates with big spoonfuls of beef or goat curry, Destini would bring out rice, and Devi would bring a pot of yellow dhal to ladle above or on the side. Fatima would bring roti, usually always dhal puri or oil roti made special with ghee, and, of course, napkins. All the girl cousins paid close attention to make sure the elders were content: "Yes, uncle, where do you want it? On the side? On top? Be careful, Uncle—it's hot!" But they also carried a reluctance and bother in their body language and something you could even hear in their voice if you listened carefully, but I don't think the uncles or the aunties really knew how to listen.

Something wasn't right. I was there, but I wasn't. I was not quite with the girl cousins, and I didn't like sitting on the floor with the boy cousins. And when I got up to help, I will always remember what happened next. Out of nowhere, Aunty Shazia, a middle aunty from Queens I didn't see often, grabbed my little shoulder and, with a stern voice, scolded me, "nah-uh, you go sit down before somebody guh talk." And she eyed me back to my place on the floor. And yee high, just taller than the counter; I had no clue what she meant. But there was a little me, confused, scared, and hurt. Did I do something wrong? How did I vex the aunties? It's not good to anger them. What does it mean for someone to "talk?" What are they gonna say?

Twenty or so years later, I know now.

"Antiman."

She didn't have to say it. But I knew she thought it, and that's why she was always cold with me, even before I knew it myself. Even before I had the words to my truth that always existed even when I was crawling on the floor with a pacifier in my mouth. It was a truth they were too ignorant to appreciate, a truth I think most of them wanted to change, and some did try. Though, some couldn't even see it right before their eyes—they were so oblivious, or maybe it was their denial and refusal to see.

That day at the reading, something wasn't right. I wasn't with girl cousins giving out food, and I wasn't sitting bored with the boy cousins. I was somewhere in between. I vehemently opposed being the boy cousin for whom they saw me. But I wasn't quite a girl cousin, not a girl like them.

Antiman. Our Guyanese word carries the weight, hate, and pain of "faggot." It's a punch to the gut, a dagger that slices me open for my blood to run out until my veins are dry and empty and my soul is lifeless. You are that other, that other the British taught us to hate. You do not belong.

I know that's probably what most of them thought.

"Faizal got he dat antiman piknee. Nah havf shame, gyul."

Is that what they all whisper and speak into the phone receiver when they do their rounds of calls over tea on the veranda?

That's why I can't bring myself today to sit on the sheets with them in a circle and eat sirnee out of a Ziploc bag because they'll see they're not wrong. That's why, no matter how many phone calls I make or postcards I send, I can't bring myself to sit in the kitchen with Big Aunty and Middle Aunty and sweat over the karahee together ... at least not dressed as me.

"Faizal got he dat antiman piknee. Nah havf shame, gyul."

But I can't dress as a stranger I don't know, with an internal light half dim, more dead than alive, pretending to be someone else.

Antiman. Literally "aunty" and "man" in English.

As a piknee, I sat in the kitchen watching my aunties do magic in their karahees. Since I was a piknee, there was always a little girl inside me who wanted to be an aunty. She grew up. She lived. They grew up, and they grew up to be an aunty. He died... well, not exactly—he never lived. And they sweat over a karahee parching flour in ghee for sirnee, chunkaying masala for curry, burning sugar to stew oxtail, and frying plantain, pholourie, and bake in bubbling oil.

I was born to grow up to be an aunty, not a man.

The year I moved to Canada was also the year I first saw Guyana. When they came to New York in the '70s and '80s, the old people dem all acquired karahees and stories they continue to carry together. To this day, they all have those utensils or miscellaneous items from back home in Guyana, some they brought with them and others they bought over here. Living in a new country, blessed to live alone in a Montreal 3½, with no roommate and no family of five in a studio apartment, there was a nostalgia I needed to live out and acquire as my own. There were rituals I needed to repeat, my own rites of passage. My own memories of a distant past. My own items from a back-home, now distanced with more time, back-homes, and space between. My own carrying and my own inheritance from a land and from those old people dem. Under the beaming sun, where time slows and the waves of the brown-water ocean crash into the mangroves and the rivers flow deep into the Amazon, I discovered my homeland under the mango trees, and I saw the little house on stilts in the village, maybe a two-bedroom or three-bedroom, where Ajee raised two hands' fingers worth of children, fed them, and Ajaa, out of a karahee, sweated over the chulha, fire side. I saw a Guyana that was the glue between every image my mind carried from all the stories the old people dem told. But I also saw a Guyana that none of them could tell me about. I saw a Guyana I had to tell them about.

I needed my own karahee and my own iron tawa too, the old Guyana-style ones you don't find the same way in stores in Canada and the United States. Everything these days comes imported from India or China, and they're just not the same, not the same style, they don't have the same shape, and they don't carry the same memory. Taximan Uncle George had been driving since all my family left Guyana. The several days before, he got to know me more, a reliable driver taking me here and there, past the old, burgundy red and white, wooden clock tower over Stabroek Market, but he only knew me dressed up as someone I don't recognize. He was a tall and kind-moustached man, maybe a few years younger than my father. I told him I needed to find a karahee and tawa.

"You guh reach," he said. "They'll sell it in Town."

Driving along the coast, past the brown water and the sea wall, the Kitty traffic circle, past the KFC, the Church's Chicken, and Popeye's, walking through Georgetown, store after store, no tawa, no karahee. Uncle George walked me along Regent Street into all the little shops, one right after another, and we asked.

And they asked us back, "what dat?"

What do you mean, "what's that?"

A karahee. A tawa. Sacred instruments our aunties carry. The vessels for any one of our multiple, beloved national dishes. I was shocked. My first time in Guyana, and some of the first Guyanese I had met, couldn't envision the simple, but magical apparatuses that transported me to Guyana for over twenty years before I came to the country.

Was this the same Guyana? Was I not Guyanese in this Guyana? How could it be the same Guyana that my family left 45 years ago? How could it be the same in Guyana?

For a moment, I thought maybe "karahee" was a word specific to Indian Guyanese, but surely all Guyanese knew a tawa. All Guyanese eat curry, but maybe not all call the pot it is cooked in a "karahee." All Guyanese who eat curry have to eat it with roti, if not rice. And all Guyanese who eat wheat, no matter where their ancestors came from, had to eat roti, and roti had to be cooked on a tawa. But the shopkeepers were Indian Guyanese.

"Oh, you mean like what dem ol' people use? A curry pot? A roti pan?"

And store after store, there was no karahee and no tawa, or they walked me down the aisle to something imported from India or China, the same thing they sell in the Indian stores in New York in a different shape, a different style, a different form, something not Guyanese that doesn't carry the same memories and the same sentiment. They showed me something that wasn't my aunties' karahee or tawa.

When the time came for me to leave Guyana, I accepted I wouldn't be taking a karahee with me or a tawa, though I had a heart full of new memories, a phone full of pictures, and a solid knowing this was my home too. The only other Guyanese things I had with me were a bag of different masala and spices and an excessive number of Demerara sugar packets from the hotel, real Guyana gold. Even sugar was a scarcity to find in the former sugar colony, and, despite the sugar shortage, the other Guyanese thing not lacking on shelves to buy was rum. Leaving Guyana was bittersweet; I still had more than they had when they practically left with a half-empty suitcase, the clothes on their backs, and the uncertainty of when and how they'd ever return. Many of them never did.

Sitting in the cramped plane seat, I woke up from a deep sleep after a short flight of an hour and a half somewhere unfamiliar but familiar, but somewhere that isn't my home: Trinidad and Tobago, somewhere my bloodlines knew just like I know the sound of sweet, sweet soca and the "mmmmm" of doubles and curry-and-cumin-covered channa spilling out between two pieces of fried dough we call "bara" on Liberty or Flatbush Avenue, or in NDG, CDN, or LaSalle. Five to seven generations back, two of my "Indian"-born ancestors were indentured here before some ship trafficked them to the Demerara Colony to be indentured again for another five-year sentence to work the plantations. The jahajis who were jahajied again were those few unlucky coolies indentured here and there and taken somewhere else to do it all over again. Essequibo, Demerara, and Berbice, or later British Guiana. Malaya. Jamaica. Fiji. Guadeloupe. Mauritius. Cape Colony. Martinique. Suriname. Réunion. Saint Vincent. British Honduras or Belize.

The list keeps on going and started even before them with the Middle Passage. Even today, those who pick your apples and package your precut steak and skinless chicken breasts in Ontario and New Jersey came from across borders. And what about those who stitch your jeans in Bangladesh and Vietnam for pennies or those who dig for lithium for your phone's battery in Bolivia and are robbed of their water? And what about those buried in collapsing cobalt mines in Congo-Kinshasa?

Somebody's child. Somebody's sibling. Somebody's parent. Somebody who will grow old to be a grandparent and great-grandparent. A human soul that loved and was loved, who cried and laughed. Somebody from lineages and cultures was carried no matter where they were trafficked and taken. Somebody who was treated as a commodity, subhuman, and a cog in a conveyor belt to fill some greedy bastard's pockets. The plantation repeats itself, thrives, and lives on. Who are those exploited? What do they carry? How do they labor? Where? Commanded, never asked, never thanked, just done.

***

When I arrived in Port of Spain from Guyana, Georgetown felt small. Turning 360 degrees and capturing the big city, Spanish and British colonial architecture, urban planning, and street names collided into one, framed by hills running into mountains traversing the island. This was no longer the British-Dutch South America I knew grounded to a continent.

When I arrived in Port of Spain from five days in Guyana,

my first five days of Guyana;

my first five days of speaking nothing but Creolese,

learning Caribbean English, and forgetting Americana;

my first five days of "good night" is a starting point and greeting

and not a "farewell,"

when I arrived in Port of Spain from Guyana, the Trinbagonians sang to me in the time my ear acclimated. When I arrived in Port of Spain from Guyana, a Trinbagonian turned to me puzzled and asked, "where's your exotic accent from?" all while they traveled up and down an octave.

In Trinidad and Tobago, there was no Taximan Uncle George, but a Driver, Uncle Johnny. When I first met Uncle Johnny, I dressed funny and spoke funny; I wasn't myself. I don't quite remember when or how I came to realize, but Uncle Johnny and I shared a lifelong survival skill of acting, acting as a stranger we don't know or recognize, a total alien, albeit we came to our acting from different sides of the stage of gender. And I emphasize Uncle not just for Guyanese, Trinbagonian honorifics, but an Uncle I since chose, an Uncle I send a voice message to wishing him "Merry Christmas," and an uncle who sends me pictures of him and the Trini tantie-uncles, Black, Indian, Chinese, and White in kurtas throwing powder for Phagwah or Holi. He's an old Uncle who gasped when he saw my pictures from deep in the past and said, "a female illusionist!" He's an old uncle who knows the words, "are you a friend of Dorothy?" He's become the uncle to send me Alok comedy sketches and deep thoughts on "they/them." He's the Uncle I bring maple syrup to from the Tobique First Nation.

At the start of the day, Uncle Johnny drove under the big green letters reading "St. James," the portal into the district where Nicki Minaj's clan hailed from and where many of the Guyanese who came to the island came to first settle. We stood up at a corner on Western Main Road, buying doubles from an aunty who wore her braids in an updo. For the breakfast of champions, out of a cooler, she took pieces of golden bara, ever so slightly dyed with turmeric but still off-white and palish yellow, and bathed the fried dough with chickpeas swimming in a sauce of spices, spooned right out of the karahee she balanced over a shopping cart. She topped it off with tamarind chutney, citrusy green chadon benni sauce, orange pepper sauce, and a white-to-green gradient of cucumber slices. I lost track of how many doubles I ate. Back in Montreal or New York, even the ones I had in Toronto didn't come close to the excellence I was blessed with those glorious days in Trinidad and Tobago.

Recharged and nourished to start the day, we got back into the car, and Uncle Johnny asked, "how was Guyana?" I told him how I couldn't get my karahee and tawa. His eyes met mine in the rearview mirror of the little sedan.

"Gyal, we got to change that today!"

Showing me the island, he diverted from the original itinerary and drove into a parking lot in Central, outside of Chaguanas. And, stepping out of the car, we walked into a huge supermarket, big like the one in Giftland Mall I was in the days before I came to this country, big and air-conditioned like any supermarket in North America. We walked past the many aisles, and a store employee took us to one towards the back. And my eyes lit up to see shelves of karahees, tawas, and more.

Karahees, tawas, and belnas of all sizes, dark iron and silver aluminum, and all true in shape and form to the ones long known in these sister lands of Trinidad and Tobago and Guyana. They had ittie-bittie karahees from 8" in diameter to big ones over 20" or more. They had big tawas and average-sized tawas. The karahees and tawas you need to feed the masjid after Jummah prayer or to feed the mandir after the pooja. They had the karahees and tawas to be an entrepreneur out of your yard, selling to your neighbors, in a restaurant, or in a food truck on the Savannah. I wanted several of each, but I was limited by how heavy my suitcase was allowed to get and how many of the white, grey, red, and blue TTD polymer notes I carried. My own aunty karahee and my own aunty tawa, not in Guyana, but here on the island of Trinidad.

Uncle Johnny took a picture of me holding them up with glee, and we tossed the bags in the trunk of his car before seeing the giant Hanuman murti standing tall into the sky and the Temple by the Sea with the jhandi flags worshippers placed into the ground nearby. Uncle Johnny that night introduced me to his friends and showed me the queers of POS, and naturally, he was the one to take me to the airport, where we said "goodbye."

Having checked in my luggage at the Copa Airlines desk, I went through passport control departing the Republic of Trinidad and Tobago. At this late in the night, Piarco Airport felt like a ghost town, so different from what I saw when I first arrived. There was still more than an hour I had to wait before boarding began at 3 o'clock in the morning. I placed my carry-on suitcase and my backpack carrying my most valuable belongings on the conveyor belt, walked through the metal detector, and waited on the other side of the X-ray machine.

And, out of nowhere, came a deep, booming voice: "which one of the aunties have di karahee and tawa in the bag?"

The voice didn't sing like the other Trinbagonian voices I heard—it just howled with authority in the witching hours of night.

"Which one of the aunties have di karahee and tawa in the bag?"

The people on the line looked around and then at me as I stuck my hand up in the air.

"I have the karahee and tawa. That's my bag."

I was the aunty, standing nearly six feet tall in jeans with stubble growing back on my face below my N95 mask with my hair tied back into a bun. I was the aunty with the karahee and tawa in my bag, though I didn't look anything like they imagined an aunty to be.

"You can't take this on the plane."

"But… but… I need my karahee and tawa with me."

"No, no, you haffi go back and put it in your checked luggage. Better hope they didn't put it on the plane yet."

My palms began to sweat as I walked with all my bags, flustered.

"Nuh dat way, di udda way." He pointed down the corridor at the end, which I walked through a few days before when I deplaned coming from Guyana.

I ran to find my checked luggage back at the Copa Airlines desk downstairs before security, and my heart raced, wondering if I would lose my dear karahee and tawa and be forced to leave them behind in Trinidad. My mind raced with fear. I was afraid they'd bring me to a room to grill me with questions to ask why. I was afraid I'd have to explain why I was the aunty taking the karahee and tawa on the plane. I was afraid I would have to explain to people in uniform why I don't look like what an aunty taking a karahee and tawa on a plane should look like or why I don't look like an aunty but my names on my passport do. Despite a few side eyes and teeth kissing at an ungodly hour, no one would want to be awake, I was fine. And, by mere luck, my suitcase wasn't yet on the plane, and even with the karahee and tawa now stuffed inside, my suitcase drifted away on a conveyor belt with no overweight fee, as if nothing had ever happened. I eventually deplaned far away in North America, and now my karahee and tawa sit heavenly on my kitchen shelf in Montreal. These are my tools, along with my techno-coolie futurism karahee. I plug into the wall, airfryer, and pressure cooker, all in one. I fry my masala down, and now I add a little methi or fenugreek leaves I find in the Indian shop, sometimes dried mint I find from the Maghrebi butcher, and, even here and there, bandhaniya, culantro, or chadon benni I buy under the name "ngò gai" from the Vietnamese supermarket. In my simple but long, flowy, floral aunty frock, I tell my friends to wash their hands and "come, come nah and eat!"

This is my aunty karahee, one of my aunty karahees, one of the many I will carry, one of the many that will carry me home faraway, bring home to home, whether I be far or near, new or long in the place I reside. So long as I have a karehee, I am home. It's the aunty karahee I will cook in when Uncle Johnny comes to visit Canada. And maybe one day, the aunties will be cooking with me, sweating over my karahees all together again, a next aunty amongst them.

KIRAN MAHARAJ

Atlantic

Of Atlas, we are drawn to the strength of the Atlantic.
So sit with me, then, observe off Florida's shores, Atlantic.

Or maybe one could speak of the leatherback turtles
that make their home in Trinidad, laying eggs from the Atlantic.

Do people even know—rather, care—of the history here? Of
lives lost, when one sought a new home in the Atlantic.

Ask the losers, the liars, the bastards, the thieves, if they
would cross from country to country like I did, facing the Atlantic.

Would they light a candle for my pain, or would they
ridicule how I've "fled from home" across the Atlantic?

Hibiscus Picking, Five a.m., 2002.

I remember waking up at 5 in the morning,
finding you sat at the same recliner,
and you asked if I wanted to go pick some flowers.

We would walk down Caroni Savannah Road,
whiling away hours on uneven pavement;
the roads would be hell on my ankles now,

with their twists and cracks.
We walked and talked about the most banal things:
about television and cricket, why I shouldn't tell my teachers

that my Nana will come slap them and how it looked on you,
and later, why I felt trepidation in attending school.
You taught me instead, that love can be trapped inside

of words. How saying *grandpa* doesn't have the same
heart to it as saying *Nana.* How saying that a person is
gone, doesn't necessarily mean that I can accept it.

If I were honest with myself, I would say that even now,
it stings terribly to not think of the person who
taught me how to curl my "join-up" *h*:

a slow rise, gentle curl, then a quick flourish.
I remember coming out from El Dorado South to find
you sitting in your old Volvo. We went down the hill,

snuck away cupcakes while Kavesh was at his lessons.
"Don't tell your Nani," you'd say, biting into it with glee.
You only ever saw me harassing Keshav,

poking his arm or riling his temper with a poor joke;
later, asking who he likes, not what he likes,

but you never saw me kiss his forehead goodnight.

You never saw my tears when the funeral pyre lit, or when
I struggled to put these words on the page for the thousandth time.

I remember waking up at 5 in the morning,
finding your ghost in the same recliner,

and it's been ten years since I've ever picked a flower.

Chai Powder

An elderly woman sits by
the window, brown hair puffed
and brushed exactly how she
always liked it— for over
forty years, she's done it the
same way. Her skin, browned
by Caribbean sun and genetics,
sags slightly. So does her smile
once her family leaves a quiet
house in Florida. She sips her
chai that she'd painstakingly
made from chai powder. Hers
to enjoy, she thinks, until a loud
voice carries through the house.
"Nani, I'm home." A grandson,
once shy, now boisterous around
her, holds her tight and steals a sip.
Her smile grows, and he asks about
her day. They sit together, sharing
tea and stories until the lonely
Florida sun sets.

Kali Ma

A hibiscus
sat by the family puja room:
We got it from the flower shop on Wiles Rd with Nani.
We said "Hello" to her husband in the picture between
Kali and Hanuman. She told me, as she always does,
that she felt his presence around me, protecting me. That

every time I say I'm home, she knows that he is home as well.

Chrysanthemum, Pinned to a Purple Sari

Set the stage for me, Auntie.

> Tell me, in your accent mixed of Piccadilly Park and Port-
> of-Spain, how you and your family lived in Cumuto, not
> sure what your futures looked like. How you were married
> off to a man you never met, like your ancestors too, but Nani,
> your sister was to remain in Caroni instead with her husband.

Bring me to Valsayn, Auntie.

> Tell me that the doubles we had from the same fellow down
> the street was just a bit too spicy, again; that the channa we
> shared had a bit too much pepper in it. How we should
> study for exams and get a chance to work in the real world
> because you and my Nani never had that opportunity.

Travel the world again, Auntie.

> Go back and forth between London and Trinidad, tell
> my Nani that you love her and call her landline, only
> so she won't pick up again. Not because Nani passed
> away, but because she's passed out. Light a candle one
> more time, at The Abbey of Our Lady of Exile, please.

Before the cancer took you Auntie,

> We sat in cheap plastic chairs after Diwali Nagar
> that you got at the market so we could gossip, show
> you how to use your phone for the hundredth time.
> You sat in your favourite purple sari and we recorded
> voice notes, sent them and said I love you, I miss you.

Lolapaka

The dark is no place
for somebody to be
alone. Dear Yama, show

me that which I cannot
see. Show me, I ask of
you, the mercy you meted

to a man who beat his
children; a man who
screamed at his wife;

a man who never learned
to tell his grandchildren
that he loved them even

on his deathbed. Show me
everything you intended for
him, even if it hurts me.

VINOD BUSJEET

Notes Towards the Definition of Culture

I.

At the hotel's Hospitality Desk, she offers me a glass of water.
On her badge, the name of a Biblical prophet.
"Leaving us on your birthday?"
she says as she hands my passport to a clerk.

"You may pick it up in two hours. You've been to our island before?"
Vicariously, through your most famous compatriot, V. S. Naipaul.
"We don't like him."
He's a master of English prose.
"He knows nothing about us. This country is not Indian."

Your Indians don't like him either: too Anglo, an apologist of Empire.
"I'm not talking of Empire, but of this country's culture."
I thought you are multicultural. Calypso, Chutney music, Roti.

II.

The doorbell rings, she gives me back my passport.
She has the gait and allure of the Queen of Sheba.
At the edge of the bed, she pulls my hands
to her shoulders, presses. "I'm going through a hellish divorce."
Surprised fingers knead.

Our evenings at Vini Mangé take me home
to sultry verandas, Creole cuisine, and vindaloo.
She introduces me to the delights of callaloo,
and to her friends, who invite me to next year's carnival,
call me a rootless cosmopolitan and criticize V. S. Naipaul.

III.

On the day of my departure, she is not at her desk.
At checkout, the cashier hands me a perfumed parcel.
I open it: a birthday card and V. S. Naipaul's *The Mystic Masseur.*

Photograph by Andil Gosine

ABOUT THE CONTRIBUTORS

Jay Aja (they/he) is nonbinary, queer, and a second-generation immigrant Guyanese. He is currently an MFA candidate in nonfiction at the University of South Florida, yet paradoxically, he mainly writes poetry and draws comics. Jay is fascinated by the confluence point of text and image, how the two in tandem may lead to more nuanced storytelling, and how these mediums may allow them to continue exploring the diaspora identity of Caribbeans within and outside the United States. Jay is currently working on a graphic memoir that navigates the effects of childhood sexual trauma alongside gender identity in a West Indian household. You can find them on Instagram and Twitter @comicsbhaijay.

Kazim Ali is the author of more than twenty books of poetry, fiction, essay, and cross-genre work. He has translated books by Ananda Devi, Marguerite Duras, and Sohrab Sepehri. He is the chair of the Department of Literature at the University of California, San Diego.

Andre Bagoo's latest books include *The Undiscovered Country, The Dreaming* and *Narcissus*. He lives in Trinidad with his dog, Chaplin.

N. Nardina Bi is a young trans writer whose work spans across short story, poetry, personal narrative, biomythography, and translations. They are a settler in Tiohtià:ke/Mooniyang (Montreal, Canada) of Indo-Guyanese and Sicilian origins. Nardina's artistry is inspired by the intersections and complexities of living trans and racialized experiences; living across borders and their family's migration narratives; unpacking the profound and rich complexities of creolization; and understanding the antiquity and vibrancy of transness and queerness around the world. They find inspiration in the diverse makeup of today's Caribbean Basin and southern Americas and in seeing just how much the Caribbean Sea connects the region's people more than it separates. They seek to use the arts to heal lineages and to build diasporic kinships through and across language(s).

Vinod Busjeet is the author of *Silent Winds, Dry Seas* (Doubleday, Penguin Random House, 2021), a novel that incorporates seven poems. Born on the island of Mauritius, he was educated at the Royal College Secondary School, then studied in Madagascar at the French Université Charles de Gaulle, and holds degrees from Wesleyan University (Connecticut), New York

University, and Harvard. He has worked as a secondary school teacher in Mauritius, an international development banker at the World Bank and the International Finance Corporation in Washington, D.C., and a diplomat. He resides in Washington, D.C., and holds dual citizenships—the United States and Mauritius. His paternal ancestor left India for Mauritius in 1853 and his maternal ancestor in 1873, the former to work as an indentured laborer on a sugar cane plantation, the latter for the Mauritius Railways Department.

Will Depoo is a versatile writer and poet whose works delve into a wide array of themes. His writings are known to explore topics such as cuisine, gender dynamics, heritage, immigration, indentured servitude, law enforcement, and substance abuse, to name a few. Will exhibits a fondness for composing in Creolese, the language native to Guyana. Will's Guyanese heritage is deeply rooted; he resided in Guyana as a young child and became proficient in Creolese during his stay. Moreover, he is a longstanding resident of East New York, Brooklyn. In addition to his creative pursuits, Will is an active organizer, dedicating his efforts to many causes. His organizing efforts encompass issues related to housing justice, tenants' rights, the fight against contemporary redlining practices, criminal justice reform, and advocacy for immigrant rights. Furthermore, Will's talent as a poet has garnered recognition, with three of his poems being published in the print edition of Gasher Press's "Cherry Moon" in 2023. His unique ability to blend his cultural heritage, community activism, and poetic expression makes him a distinctive and impactful voice in the literary and social justice landscapes.

Ananda Devi is the 2024 recipient of the Neustadt Prize, known as the "American Nobel." She is the author of numerous volumes of short fiction and poetry, as well as novels and memoirs. Her novel *Eve de ses décombres* won the Prix des cinq continents de la Francophonie in 2006, as well as several other prizes, and was adapted for the cinema by Sharvan Anenden and Harrikrisna Anenden. She has since won other literary prizes, including the Prix Louis Guilloux for Le Sari Vert, the Prix Ouest France Étonnants Voyageurs for Manger L'autre, and the Prix Femina des lycéens for Le rire des déesses. For the totality of her work, she received the Prix du Rayonnement de la langue et de la littérature française of the Académie française, and in 2010, she was named Chevalier des Arts et des Lettres by the French Government. In 2023, she was awarded both the Prix de la langue française and the Neustadt Prize, cementing her reputation as a leading voice in French and world letters.

Gitan Djeli is a Mauritian writer and researcher in cultural studies. Her creative work appears in *The Funambulist, Doek!, adda, Poetry* and in the anthology *We Mark Your Memory* by Commonwealth Writers, among others.

Ari Gautier is a French-speaking author born in Madagascar to a Franco-Tamil father and a Malagasy mother. He spent his childhood in his father's native country of Pondicherry, India. Then, as an adult, he lived between Paris and Pondicherry before settling in Oslo. Author of two novels, *Carnet Secret de Lakshmi* (2015) and *Le Thinnai* (2017), as well as a collection of short stories, *Nocturne Pondichéry* (2021). Ari Gautier's goal and ambition are to put Pondicherry on the world literary map. He encourages and helps his compatriots to write and publish their own stories.

Andil Gosine is professor of environmental arts and justice at York University in Toronto and author of *Nature's Wild: Love, Sex and Law in the Caribbean.* Since 2014, he has led the research project "Visual Arts After Indenture," which has resulted in many exhibitions, including *Coolie Coolie Viens, Everything Slackens in a Wreck, Wendy Nanan* and *Kelly Sinnapah Mary*, at various museums and galleries in the Americas, and numerous publications, including special issues of *Small Axe* and *Wasafiri.*

C. Govender writes narrative nonfiction.

Kevin Jared Hosein is an author and science teacher from Chaguanas in Trinidad. He won the Caribbean regional prize in the 2015 Commonwealth Short Story Prize, and in 2018, his story "Passage" was the winner of the overall Commonwealth Short Story Prize. He is the author of three books published in the Caribbean, and his novel *Hungry Ghosts* was published in 2023 by Bloomsbury in the United Kingdom and Ecco in America. His short fiction and essays have been featured in numerous outlets, including *BBC Radio 4, Wasafiri, Granta, Lightspeed Magazine, Perspective*, and *The Big Issue.*

Ajith Kanna has been teaching French for over twenty-four years. He has taught French at various institutions while working as a permanent faculty member at the Central Institute of English and Foreign Languages (CIEFL), Lucknow, Uttar Pradesh, India (now named English and Foreign Languages University [EFLU]) from 1999 to 2004. He joined Jawaharlal Nehru University (JNU), New Delhi, in May 2004, and in September 2014, he became a full professor. He has translated some of Periyar's essays from Tamil to English and French. His other publications in translation include: (i) *Caste Must Be Destroyed. Why?* (from Tamil to English); (ii) *Les castes doivent être détruites. Pourquoi?* (from Tamil to French); (iii) *La libération de l'ignorance est la vraie libération pour les arundathiyars* (from Tamil to French); (iv) *Tragedy of Appasamy or an Amazing Story of a Traveler* (from French to English); (v) *A Buried Path* (from Tamil to English); (vi) *Un Chemin enterré* (from Tamil to French). His next book is *A Mother's Diary.* This is translated from a collection of short stories in Tamil titled அம்மாவின் டைரி/*Ammāviṉ ṭairi/*, and was launched on August 25,

2023. He has also published the *Advanced Learners' English Grammar Book* and a text book in French for beginners.

Kiran Maharaj received his MFA from Emerson College and was the recipient of the MFA Scholarship for Excellence in Writing at Emerson College. He now works with the TESS group at MIT. His poetry has been featured in *Magpie Literary Journal* and *Gnashing Teeth Publishing*'s Hallowscream.

Renluka Maharaj was born in Trinidad and Tobago and works between Colorado, New York City and Trinidad. She attended the University of Colorado, Boulder where she earned her BFA, and her MFA at The School of The Art Institute of Chicago. Some of her works are in the collections of The Art Institute of Chicago, Flaten Museum and Bank of America. Her work has also appeared in publications such as *Elle India, Harper's Bazaar India, New American Paintings, Coolitude Volume II, Juxtapoz, Hyperallergic*, and *Nourish and Resist* (anthology of Caribbean Literature).

Born in Suva, Fiji, **Sudesh Mishra** is a professor of literature at the University of the South Pacific. He has previously worked at universities in Australia (Flinders University and Deakin University) and Britain (University of Stirling). He has been the recipient of an Australian Research Council Postdoctoral Fellowship, the Harri Jones Memorial Prize for Poetry, an Asialink Residency in India, the Ratu Sir Kamisese Mara Fellowship (Otago University), and an Erskine Canterbury Fellowship (Canterbury University). He is the author of five books of poems, including *Tandava* (Meanjin Press: Melbourne University, 1992), *Diaspora and the Difficult Art of Dying* (Otago UP, 2002), and *The Lives of Coat Hangers* (Otago UP, 2016). He has completed a draft of his sixth volume.

Nadia Misir is a writer who was born, raised, and is still living in South Ozone Park, Queens. Her writing has been published in *Poetry, Kweli, Papercuts, Open City Magazine*, and *No, Dear Magazine*. Her creative practice has been supported by fellowships from the Asian American Writers' Workshop, the Louis Armstrong House Museum, the Jamaica Center for Arts and Learning, and QCVoices. She has facilitated writing workshops in collaboration with the School of Making Thinking, the South Asian Feminism(s) Alliance, Queens Memory, Reimagine, the Five Boro Story Project, and others. She received her BA in English from SUNY Oswego and an MA in American studies from Columbia University. She also holds an MFA in fiction writing from Queens College, CUNY. She is in transit more often than she is at home. Her tuxedo cat, Keto, is her favorite furry alarm clock.

Poet, memoirist, and translator, **Rajiv Mohabir**, is the author of four books of poetry, including *Whale Aria* (Four Way Books, 2023) and *Cutlish* (Four Way Books, 2021), which was a finalist for the National Book Critics Circle

Award and recipient of the Eric Hoffer Medal Provocateur. His poetry and nonfiction have been finalists for the 2022 PEN/America Open Book Award, the Lambda Literary Award in Poetry and in Nonfiction, the Randy Shilts Award for Gay Nonfiction, and both second place and finalist for the Guyana Prize for Literature in 2022 (poetry and memoir, respectively). His translations won the Harold Morton Landon Translation Award from the American Academy of Poets in 2020. He is an assistant professor of poetry at the University of Colorado, Boulder.

As a Geet/Ghazal/Bhajan/Pop singer, composer, singer-songwriter, and poet, **Raj Mohan** has been established as the finest Sarnámi artist in the Netherlands and Surinam for the last thirty years. As a singer and poet in the Sarnámi-Bhojpuri language, he travels to Suriname, French Guyana, South Africa, Mauritius, India, and several European countries to perform. In 2011, he wrote and composed his first pop album in Sarnámi-Bhojpuri, which includes Hindi songs and poems. It is the first time in Surinamese history that the Sarnámi-Bhojpuri has been utilized in this contemporary form. Raj Mohan invented the Sarnámi-Bhojpuri Geet in the Geet and Ghazal style, which was appreciated worldwide with his album, *Kantráki* (2005). The Geet/Ghazalnuma songs are performed by Raj in the traditional Ghazal setting as well as in jazz and pop (Album: *Daayra*, 2011). He released five music albums (a Bhajan album with Shri Anup Jalota) and two books with Sarnámi-Bhojpuri poems. His latest album, *Dui Mutthi* (2013), was released on the 140th anniversary of the Indian migration to Suriname.

Nicholas Augustus Peters is a writer and professional in the areas of human rights and development. He has a special interest in issues related to social movements and decolonization. He is a proud graduate of the University of Guyana with a Bachelor of Arts in English Literature and Linguistics. His subsequent experience as a journalist and in civil society led him to pursue his postgraduate studies in 2018. That year, he was awarded the Chevening Scholarship to study for his Master of Arts in Human Rights at the University of Sussex. Nicholas's interest in writing was propelled by the 2016 Walter Rodney Creative Writing Competition, hosted by the University of Guyana. His entry, *A Centuries Old Flame*, won the fiction category. The story explored Guyana 100 years after their independence from British colonialism, where the wealth of the nation is defined by its petrochemical bounty. He explored themes of exploitation, neocolonialism, and the rising tensions in the Guyanese sociopolitical environment. Nicholas continues to experiment with his writing in prose and, more recently, with poetry. Upon his return to Guyana, Nicholas worked with the United Nations Migration Agency—the International Organization for Migration. He currently works at the Amerindian Peoples Association as the Advocacy and Policy Officer.

Alisha Prasad is an Auckland-based graphic designer from Aotearoa, New Zealand, who has a passion for meaningful storytelling through graphic design. She specializes in branding, identity, illustration, and publication design. Her creative process places importance on every step of the journey, from the conception of a complex idea to the execution of a strong and impactful finished product. Alisha studied at Auckland University of Technology, where she graduated with a bachelor's degree in design, majoring in communication design. She is now working as a professional graphic designer with over two years of commercial experience. As a proud Indo-Fijian creative, Alisha often draws from her rich cultural background and surroundings within her personal projects as a source of inspiration. Aotearoa, Fiji, and India all have a vibrant and abundant visual language that comes together to influence Alisha's work. Since she was young, drawing, painting, and making have always been a passion of hers. Connecting organically to her work through her hands is an essential element of her craft. You will often see analogue drawings, paintings, as well as digital illustrations scattered throughout her work. Alisha has also won a Bronze Best Award for her capstone university project, *Yaad Karo*, from the Designers Institute of New Zealand in 2022.

Shivanee Ramlochan is a Trinidadian writer. Her debut, *Everyone Knows I Am a Haunting* (Peepal Tree Press, 2017), was shortlisted for the 2018 Forward Prize for Poetry. Recently, her poems have been anthologized in *100 Queer Poems* (Faber); *After Sylvia: Poems and Essays in Celebration of Sylvia Plath* (Nine Arches Press); *Across Borders: An Anthology of New Poetry from the Commonwealth* (Verve Poetry Press); and *Bi+ Lines: An Anthology of Contemporary Bi+ Poems* (fourteen poems). Shivanee was a 2019 John Ciardi Poetry Fellow at Bread Loaf Writers Conference; a 2019 Millay Arts Poetry alumna; and a 2020 Catapult Arts Residency awardee. She is currently the Translation Selector for the Poetry Book Society and has worked in Caribbean literary development for thirteen years. The Spanish edition of *Everyone Knows I Am a Haunting* (*Todos saben que soy una aparición*) is in development, and Shivanee's second book, *Unkillable*, on Indo-Caribbean women's disobedience, is forthcoming.

Francine Simon was born in 1990 in Durban, South Africa, to Indian Catholic parents. She holds a doctorate in English studies from Stellenbosch University. Her poetry, which has been published in South African and international literary journals, was shortlisted for the Sol Plaatje European Union Poetry Award in 2012 and received the DALRO Poetry Prize in 2016. She launched her debut collection of poetry, *Thungachi*, in 2017 and a chapbook, *SHARK*, in 2019. She lives in Northern Italy.

Chandanie Somwaru is an Indo-Caribbean woman who was born and raised in Queens, New York. She received an MFA in poetry from Queens College and is currently a Ph.D. student at the University of Hawai'i at Mānoa studying creative writing. Somwaru published a chapbook with Ghostbird Press in 2021 titled *Urgent \\ Where the Mind Goes \\ Scattered*. Previous work can be seen in *Honey Literary, Solstice, SWWIM, The Margins, VIDA Review*, and elsewhere.

PERMISSIONS

Grateful acknowledgement is made to all the authors, translators, and copyright holders for permission to publish their work. Reprints are not permitted without their written consent. The editors thank the following for permission to reprint previously published works.